ELIZABETH TAYLOR

My Celebrity Connection

WAYNE GRIFFIN

Copyright © 2024 by Wayne Griffin.

ISBN 978-1-7635651-0-4 (paperback)
ISBN 978-1-7635651-1-1 (hardback)
ISBN 978-1-7635651-2-8 (ebook)

All rights reserved. No part of this book may be reproduced or transmitted in any form or by any means, electronic or mechanical, including photocopying, recording, or by any information storage and retrieval system without express written permission from the author, except in the case of brief quotations embodied in critical reviews and certain other noncommercial uses permitted by copyright law.

Copyright of most of the images is the property of the author, other images used have granted copyright consent. While every effort has been made to contact copyright holders for consent to use some images, in some instances copyright holders have been untraceable for which we offer or sincere apologise. Such images have therefore been acknowledged in the source notation and photographic credits at the back of this book.

Printed in the United States of America.

CONTENTS

Dedication 9
Your Inaugural QR Code 10
Memorabilia 11
A Word from Sir John-Michael Howson................................12
A Word from the Author 13
Wildwood Road, Hampstead 14
Hired Help 15
A Childhood Friend 22
White Cliffs of Dover...26
A Flawless and Enchanting Portrayal....................................27
A Stroll Down the Main Street of London............................ 41
Touching Up Her Makeup 44
Autograph-Seeking Fans...46
Antique Gift 47
Mother and I...49
Beauty Regime..50
Rose Petals and Green Leaves 51
The Hiltons..58
From the Corridors of MGM 61
On Board the Queen Mary 64
A Love Affair with Jewels..65
The Diamond Look 66
Honorary President...72
The Last Time I Saw Paris 79
Raintree County 93

The Raintree County Picnic 96
Elizabeth Was Very Giving 97
An Embellished Bracelet 99
Beaumont Inn Harrodsburg 100
Elizabeth Tours Australia 107
Double-Breasted Herringbone Coat 111
A Crystal Pin Brooch 114
Elizabeth's Head Wrap 116
The Taylor-Todd Estate 118
The Hair Brush Set 119
Elizabeth's Curly Locks 120
The Clear Crystal Perfume Bottle 121
Lulu Bridal Wear 124
Debbie's Wedding Gift 126
The Elegant Black Lycra Elbow-Length Gloves 129
Gray Faux-Poodle-Fur Cape 133
Severe Bout of Pneumonia 135
The Astonishing Earrings of Elizabeth Taylor 139
The Enigmatic Elegance of Cleopatra's Gown 144
A Regal Relic from the Sets of Cleopatra 146
Marvels from the Sands of Egypt 149
Elizabeth, Poolside, 1963 154
Makeup Artist to the Stars 155
Cream Woolen Trousers 156
Enchantment in Bloom: The Lily of the Valley Wedding 158
An Unforgettable Gesture: National Velvet
Gifted by Mrs. Richard Burton 161
Mrs. Burton's Private Jet 165

A Treasured Find: Elizabeth Taylor's Personal Jewellery Case 169

The Powder-Blue Coat 172

Top Shelf Courvoisier and Hennessey 174

A Treasured Relic: Tiffany & Co. Money Clip 175

The Symbol of Everlasting Love: The Krupp Diamond 176

Hosting Hollywood Parties 180

Saks Fifth Avenue 181

Leopard Skins 182

Elizabeth in Mind 183

The Iconic Director's Chair of E. T. B 184

A Splash of Multi-Coloured Glamour..186

Victorio & Lucchino...188

Strolling the Streets in Plaid..190

A Love Story Etched in Pink 193

The Ashtray 194

Collection of Head Scarves 196

Psychedelic Flowers and Swirls 197

Gemma Taccogna 198

Entertaining Guests 199

The Persimmon Background..200

Bouquets of Violets..202

Luz Originals 203

The Embroidered Blouse 204

Elizabeth's Lavender Crystal Perfume Bottle 205

The 1972 Premiere 207

Southern Fried Chicken 209

Ritz Hotel in Paris, 1976 210

Valentino...213

The Chiffon Evening Gown	217
Butterflies and Circles	218
The Marabou House Shoes	220
Theatre World Award Party	225
Little Foxes	226
A Custom-Made Fur Collar	229
Los Angeles Airport	232
Through the Lens of Sadness	236
Madame Conti	242
Oscars Ceremony	245
Sunburst Pleat and Full-Length Ruffles	246
Spaghetti Straps that Flow to the Floor	249
The Poker Alice-Screen-Worn Shoes	256
Alice Moffit	257
Taffeta Moiré Complimented with Silk Flowers	259
Signed Alice Faux Playing Cards	261
Periwinkle Blue	263
Fashion Designer Andre van Pier	269
Matilda Otto	270
The American Hope Awards	275
The Birthday Napkin	283
Rhinestone Encrusted	286
A Personal Gift from Elizabeth	288
Santa Monica	292
Elizabeth's Fabulous Sweater	301
The Lavender Satin-and-Rhinestone Clutch	309
A Dream Come True	312
The Violet and Pink Belts	313

Happy Birthday	315
Elizabeth Emmanuel	316
Elizabeth Has a Fancy Tunic	323
Rhinestone Checkers	324
These Old Broads	328
Ostrich Feathers	331
Memorabilia	334
Elizabeth's Last Public Outing	338
The Lavender Manuscript	339
Such an Extensive Volume	341
Cedar-Sinai Medical Centre	343
In Memoria	348
A Homage to Elizabeth	353
A Celebrity Connection Immortalised	358
700 Nimes Road	366
Some More Photographic Credits	369
A Special Mention	370

DEDICATION

To the lady whom without a doubt is the perfect essence of true celebrity, Elizabeth, thank you for adding endless hours of joy, excitement, and passion to our world, and without whom, this celebrity connection could never have been made possible.

My heart brims with gratitude for the boundless joy, exhilaration, and fervour you have infused into my world.

Without your luminous presence, this divine connection to celebrity would remain an unattainable dream.

I also extend my deepest appreciation to my beloved Christopher, whose unwavering support fuels my determination to persist in chasing my passions relentlessly and to Jason Trent and the team at Book Connex. Thank you for connecting my connection with celebrity to the world.

Today we remember an extraordinary tale of celebrity connection and a lifetime of unconditional and unwavering commitment to human equality.

#ElizabethTaylor#Relevant#Always.

YOUR INAUGURAL QR CODE

In recent times, the QR code has emerged as a symbol of resilience in the face of global adversity.

Within the pages of "Elizabeth Taylor My Celebrity Connection", these QR codes serve as portals, offering instant access to the enchanting world of one iconic figure: Elizabeth Taylor.

While QR codes have previously been associated with ensuring safety and preserving lives, the ones nestled within this narrative serve a different purpose—they serve as virtual gateways, breathing life into Elizabeth's story and my personal connection to her celebrity.

Behold, your inaugural QR code—an invitation to delve into the author's captivating journey and his treasured collection of memorabilia.

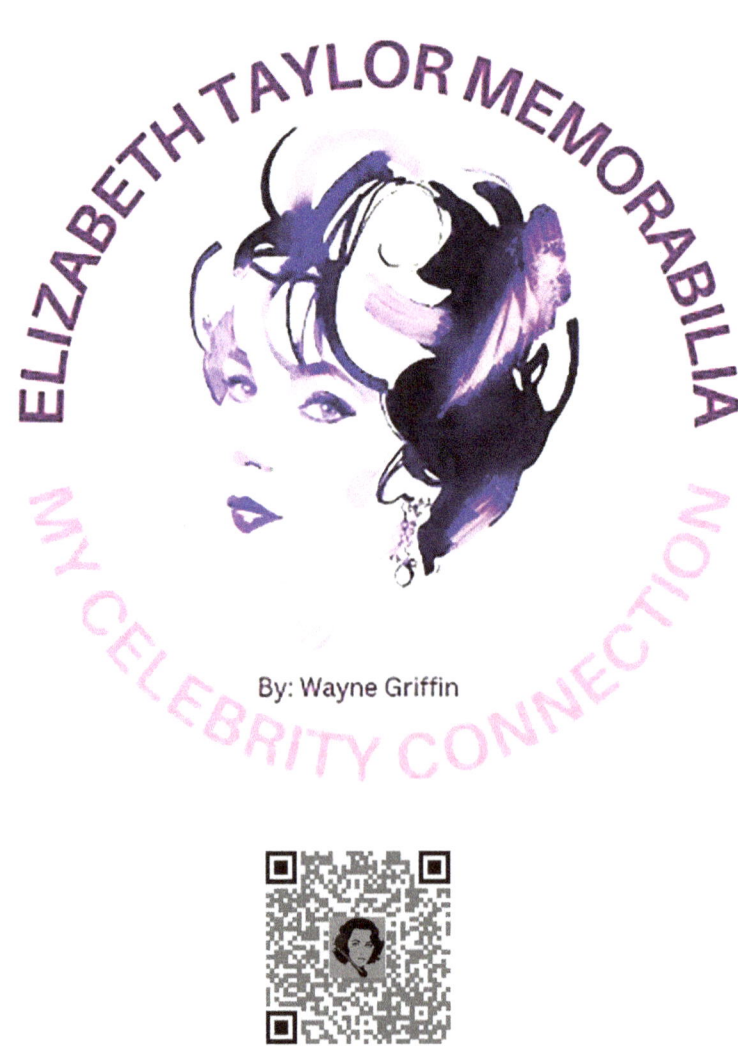

MEMORABILIA

[mem·o·ra·bil·ia]

1. Treasured possessions imbued with historical significance, cultural resonance, or ties to entertainment: encompassing items like posters, promotional photographs, and all manner of memorabilia associated with Elizabeth Taylor.
2. Commemorative moments or experiences deserving of preservation: encapsulated within a tome chronicling the lifestyle of Elizabeth Taylor and her illustrious career on the silver screen.
3. A homage to memory: an English translation that reveres the enduring legacy of Elizabeth Taylor.

Great remembrance of Dame Elizabeth Taylor

A WORD FROM SIR JOHN-MICHAEL HOWSON

Once upon a time, the word star applied to someone fabulous who worked in the entertainment business. It was an accolade for those with a magnetism, glamour, and quality that set them apart from mere mortals.

Then came the era of celebrity when the industry was created around people who were famous for being famous—fodder for the phony celebrity mill that made headlines for all the wrong reasons, none of them having anything to do with talent. So how do we describe a star that was a star and not just a headline? They became a "superstar," and when that word was devalued, we made them a "megastar."

Elizabeth—never "Liz," always Elizabeth—was not just one of the world's most beautiful and alluring women but an accomplished actor who was willing to shed the image of perfect beauty when the role required it of her. In an era when children of the rich and famous are often poster material for being troubled or in trouble, Elizabeth's family are a true testament to her role as a mother, even as her personal life made news around the world.

A star who is a real star is a person who is under the spotlight, and that's how I would describe Dame Elizabeth. When Elizabeth enters a room, you see a radiance that beguiles everyone. If you are fortunate enough to be close enough to look into those violet eyes, you can understand how so many men wilted and fell in love with her.

> "I first met the late Elizabeth in 1992 at the LA Equestrian Centre when she was launching White Diamonds. Elizabeth was extraordinarily beautiful and gracious."

By Sir John-Michael Howson, OAM

Australian author, writer, and media commentator

A WORD FROM THE AUTHOR

Get ready for a wild ride through the glitz and glamour of Hollywood's final queen, Elizabeth Taylor, in my book, "Elizabeth Taylor My Celebrity Connection."

It's not just a biography—it's a magical journey of celebrity encounters, filled with quirky tales and personal treasures that have come my way over the years.

I've been the guardian, the caretaker, if you will, of Elizabeth's essence, preserving her spirit in every fibre and mineral of her earthly possessions. Her extravagant lifestyle unfolds before you, sprinkled with anecdotes and mementos that'll make any fan feel like they're right there with her.

But my connection with Elizabeth goes beyond mere chance—it's like our lives were destined to intertwine. Imagine this: the day I entered the world, Richard Burton was busy snagging that legendary Krupp diamond for Elizabeth.

And guess what? Many of her big wins, like becoming a dame in 2000, happened on my birthday! Coincidence? I think not!

And get this—across oceans and continents, we've walked the same streets. I strolled down Wildwood Road in Mount Buller, while Elizabeth roamed the very same path in Hampstead. It's like we're connected by some cosmic thread, weaving our stories together in a way that's truly one-of-a-kind.

WILDWOOD ROAD, HAMPSTEAD

The tale of Elizabeth Taylor's beginnings traces back to the union of Francis Lenn Taylor and Sara Viola Southern in 1926. Their journey led them to welcome their first child, Howard Taylor, in 1929.

Then, at 2:15 a.m. on February 27, 1932, in a quaint cottage nestled at the end of Wildwood Road in North London, their daughter entered the world.

Elizabeth Rosemond Taylor arrived with more than just remarkable beauty—she boasted double-rowed eyelashes and those mesmerising violet eyes that would become legendary.

Born amidst the throes of the Great Depression, Elizabeth brought a beacon of love and joy to a world shrouded in darkness.

HIRED HELP

Imagine the astonishment when George and Gladys Mead Culverhouse found themselves living in close proximity to the illustrious Taylors.

In 1929, George, in desperate need of employment, scoured the local newspapers. His eyes widened in disbelief as he stumbled upon an intriguing advertisement seeking a chauffeur-handyman for a residence on none other than Wildwood Road in Hampstead, North London.

Without hesitation, George seized the opportunity and joined the Taylors' household. Little did he know, this decision would alter the course of his family's destiny forever. From the moment he set foot on the estate, George was captivated by the meticulous nature of Sara Taylor, who oversaw every aspect of the household with exacting precision.

One memorable day, as George observed Sara perched on a ladder, meticulously painting a kitchen wall, he realised the depth of her attention to detail. When Sara received a lavish gift of three hundred tulips, she entrusted George with the task of planting them precisely where she desired.

With unwavering dedication, George followed her instructions to the letter, unaware of the whimsical twist fate had in store.

Months passed, and Sara noticed tulips blooming everywhere except her garden.

Bewildered, she confronted George, who, upon investigation, unearthed a startling revelation—the tulip bulbs had been planted upside down, exactly as Sara had instructed. Despite knowing better, George had faithfully followed Sara's directives to the letter.

Undeterred by challenges, George committed himself to his duties, often toiling from dawn until the wee hours of the morning. It became a hallmark of the Taylors' refined lifestyle to rely on hired help for transportation, sparing them the indignity of driving themselves.

George was required to chauffeur them everywhere, from fashionable supper clubs to nightclubs and wealthy patronised theatres.

Sara Taylor was very artistic, and one Christmas when money was scarce, she made hand-decorated boxes out of old wooden cigar boxes.

Many of the Taylors' friends cherished such handmade delights. After much encouragement from both Sara and Francis Taylor, George and Gladys were married. Shortly after, Gladys joined her husband and was employed also by the Taylors as a cook.

They both resided in the servants' quarters, which was in the attic of the main house. By this time, the Taylor family was growing with the addition of Elizabeth and her older brother, Howard.

George continued his work as a chauffeur, handyman, gardener, and potty-emptier to Elizabeth and a storyteller to Howard.

After a while, George and Gladys wanted more privacy and were ready to raise a family, so they purchased a small house in the suburbs.

George and Gladys's daughter Ruth was born on September 24, 1934. Ruth and Elizabeth spent a lot of time together in the Taylors' house. With only two years between them, Ruth was lucky enough to receive Elizabeth's hand-me-down baby clothes, and it wasn't long before the Taylors were calling Ruth "Second-hand Rose." As a toddler, Elizabeth Taylor was always under the watchful eye of her mother.

At one point, Sara had Elizabeth taking dancing lessons, etiquette lessons, and any other lessons that would pave her future career. Sara felt a deep longing for her daughter to work in show business and knew Elizabeth had the beauty and talent to be successful, and she would not accept or tolerate anything less than perfection.

Eventually and as time passed, Ruth, even though a little girl from the wrong side of the tracks, was finally old enough to help her mum and dad around the Taylor's house. She would be invited to come along when both Gladys and George were working, and she had full use of Elizabeth and Howard's playground and toys.

The Wildwood house was a beautiful two-story brick home, kind of very similar to a Georgian style. The house backed onto the Hampstead woods, which were such a beautiful delight in spring. The house was adorned in a blanket of daffodils, and shortly after bluebells were everywhere.

Ruth would climb onto a wooden gym set, where her imagination would take over and the games with tigers, wolves, monkeys, and lions would begin.

It was good to see that someone was making the most of the wooden gym because Elizabeth and Howard hardly ever got to play, as they were always busy with private schooling and being under the watchful eye of their nanny, Frieda Gill.

Next door to 8 Wildwood Road lived several children. Their name was Kestenbaum, and they were Jewish. Sara Taylor would not let Elizabeth or Howard play with them; she had a thing for Jews, even though her maiden name was Warmbrodt and her parents were Dutch Jews.

Source: Ruth Culverhouse/ Boucher Banks *(So Blessed)*. Pictured are Gladys and George on their wedding day.

Sara Taylor
with her two-year-old daughter, **Elizabeth**, and her son, **Howard**.

Elizabeth, at three years of age, plays in her garden at the Taylors' Wildwood Road cottage in England, 1935.

Source: Gladys Culverhouse (the Taylors' maid at the time).

My brother Howard was 5½ and I was only 3½ when dad took this picture

The personal photograph

This portrait of Elizabeth and her brother, Howard, was taken by their father, Francis, in 1935.

On the reverse side of this image, Elizabeth has personally inscribed details about the photograph, including the photographer's name and the ages of herself and her brother at the time it was taken.

At the tender age of three, Elizabeth took her first steps onto the grand stage of public adoration. Draped in the delicate guise of a butterfly, she captivated audiences at Madam Vercconi's 1935 concert for the royal family.

As she fluttered gracefully, Elizabeth's enchanting presence held the crowd spellbound. Each bow she bestowed upon her audience seemed to draw them deeper into her spell, until she stood alone, the final figure bathed in applause.

In that moment, the world glimpsed the mesmerising beauty of Elizabeth Taylor, a fascination that would endure throughout her lifetime and beyond.

With the spectre of World War II looming, Sara Taylor made the courageous decision to uproot her family from England in June 1939. They embarked on a journey across the ocean to the sun-kissed hills of California, where Francis would later join them, establishing himself as a prominent art dealer at the illustrious Beverly Hills Hotel.

In a poignant snapshot frozen in time, Elizabeth, her brother Howard, and their mother Sara bid farewell to their beloved home on June 19, 1939. The image captures the essence of their departure, marking the end of an era at 8 Wildwood Road, Hampstead, North London.

A CHILDHOOD FRIEND

It would be several years before the Taylors summoned their loyal staff to join them in their newfound homeland. Among them was Ruth Culverhouse, a cherished childhood friend of Elizabeth Taylor.

In these rare and precious photographs, we catch glimpses of Ruth, captured in playful moments with her father, George, amidst the enchanting surroundings of the Taylors' Hampstead Estate in 1939.

Ruth and her family shared a special bond with the Taylors, remaining steadfast friends until the early 1950s.

As the Taylors settled into their new life and Francis Taylor established his uncle's art gallery at the prestigious Beverly Hills Hotel, they eventually moved to 703 North Elm Drive, California.

Source: Glenys and George Culverhouse, Ruth Culverhouse and Bryan Hamilton.

The journey of Elizabeth Taylor's ascent to stardom is woven with remarkable twists of fate and astonishing encounters.

Through the extensive network cultivated by Francis Taylor in his business ventures, Elizabeth found herself face-to-face with Universal's esteemed producer, John Constantine, on September 18, 1941.

With a stroke of destiny, she inked a six-month renewable contract, earning $100 per week. Thus, the stage was set for her cinematic debut.

In a whirlwind of excitement, Elizabeth stepped into the spotlight in Universal's motion picture "There's One Born Every Minute", alongside luminaries Catherine Doucette and the endearing Alfalfa Sweetzer.

However, amidst the glitz and glamour, doubts loomed. Edward Muhl, the studio's production chief, voiced scepticism, citing Elizabeth's perceived shortcomings in dancing, singing, and a premature air about her eyes. Despite this initial setback, Elizabeth's indomitable spirit shone through.

Regrettably, "There's One Born Every Minute" marked both the beginning and end of Elizabeth's tenure with Universal Pictures. Just eight months later, her contract was abruptly terminated.

However, fate had grander plans in store. Elizabeth swiftly transitioned to Metro Goldwyn Mayer (MGM), where she embarked on a new chapter as Priscilla in Fred M. Wilcox's 1943 film, "Lassie Come Home."

From this pivotal moment, Elizabeth's star blazed brightly under the MGM banner, illuminating screens for the next eighteen illustrious years. Such is the remarkable odyssey of Elizabeth Taylor's climb to cinematic greatness

Elizabeth is pictured here in her very first movie role in the film *There's One Born Every Minute.*

Elizabeth Taylor: My Celebrity Connection | 23

Best Wishes
Elizabeth Taylor

In the year that followed, Elizabeth's cinematic journey took remarkable strides as she graced the silver screen in not one, but two minor films: "The White Cliffs of Dover," opposite the talented Roddy McDowall, and Robert Stevenson's adaptation of "Jane Eyre."

However, it was her role as Velvet Brown in the 1945 MGM classic, "National Velvet," that catapulted her to unprecedented fame.

When "National Velvet" premiered on October 4, 1945, Elizabeth's luminous presence captivated audiences worldwide, transforming her into an overnight sensation.

At the tender age of twelve, Elizabeth found herself propelled into the stratosphere of stardom, commanding a staggering salary of $30,000 per year. The film's phenomenal success, grossing over $4.4 million, cemented Elizabeth's place in cinematic history.

Yet, fame often extracts a toll, and Elizabeth's ascent to stardom was not without its challenges. A harrowing fall from a horse during filming left her with severe back injuries, crushing two of her lower vertebrae. Despite the pain, Elizabeth's resilience shone through.

The studio bestowed upon her the cherished horse, King Charles, a faithful companion until his passing. However, the injuries sustained would later confine Elizabeth to a wheelchair in her twilight years.

In a poignant screen capture from the film, Elizabeth is immortalised alongside co-star Roddy McDowall, adorned in a chequered pinafore, a testament to her youthful exuberance and undeniable talent.

Elizabeth Taylor: My Celebrity Connection | 25

WHITE CLIFFS OF DOVER

Behold this captivating relic from the golden age of cinema! This chequered pinafore, worn by none other than Elizabeth Taylor herself, graced the silver screen in the 1944 masterpiece, "The White Cliffs of Dover."

Immerse yourself in the enchanting allure of this child-sized blue-and-white chequered pinafore, adorned with delicate lace trim and featuring two front pockets and butterfly-style shoulders. Its bib-style top and gracefully tied back evoke a sense of timeless elegance.

Picture young Elizabeth, a mere twelve years old, sharing the spotlight with the talented Roddy McDowall, who would later become a cherished lifelong friend. Their on-screen chemistry would later be immortalised in cinematic classics such as "Lassie Come Home" and the epic "Cleopatra."

Source: Butterfield and Butterfield auctions, USA.

26 | *Elizabeth Taylor: My Celebrity Connection*

A FLAWLESS AND ENCHANTING PORTRAYAL

This beautiful brown wig was worn by Elizabeth Taylor for her breakout role as Velvet Brown in the 1944 multiple-Oscars-winning family classic, *National Velvet*. It is hand-tied and made from human hair and includes the original Max Factor box and the MGM-wig stock-record card. The wig originated from MGM Wig Works.

Source: Manufactured by Wig Works Studios California/ MGM Studios.

HONORING OUR 21st YEAR OF LEADERSHIP
WITH A PICTURE YOU'LL BE PROUD TO PLAY
"NATIONAL VELVET

Elizabeth as Velvet Brown, flawless and enchanting portrayal...a materialized dream of wholesome loveliness.

—*The New York Times*

Elizabeth was now a star.

Source: *National Velvet* program (1945).

In 1946, Elizabeth Taylor embarked on a new chapter of her illustrious life—she penned the first of her four enchanting books. Titled "Nibbles and Me," this literary gem delved into her heartwarming bond with nine delightful pet chipmunks, weaving tales of love and companionship that enchanted readers far and wide.

Yet, even amidst the beauty of her literary endeavours, tragedy cast its shadow over the Taylor family and in November of the same year, after two decades of marriage, Sara and Francis Taylor parted ways, marking the end of an era.

Surrounded by the tumultuous backdrop of her personal life, Elizabeth's radiance continued to captivate the hearts of America.

Renowned gossip columnist Hedda Hopper, in a proclamation that echoed across the nation, hailed Elizabeth as "the most beautiful woman in America." Such was the spellbinding allure of Elizabeth Taylor, a luminary whose beauty transcended mere mortal realms.

Elizabeth's first of four books. This one was more about her nine pet chipmunks than herself (1946).

Source: Duell, Sloan & Pearce.

*Working with horses and dogs
was no great work;
it was like playing myself for two months
and the studio even gave me the horse.
—Elizabeth Taylor.*

In the midst of resounding applause and the box office success of "National Velvet," Elizabeth Taylor's stardom soared ever higher. Seizing upon her unparalleled charm and talent, filmmakers beckoned her to yet another animal-themed adventure.

This time, she shared the screen with the beloved canine, Bill, in the Fred M. Wilcox production, "Courage of Lassie."

With each role, Elizabeth solidified her status as a cinematic powerhouse—a young talent with boundless potential.

Her spellbinding performances promised a future brimming with success, leading MGM to secure her for a string of promising projects.

In a remarkable turn of events, Elizabeth found herself loaned to Warner Bros in 1947, where she embarked on two captivating journeys: "Life with Father" and the Robert Z. Leonard-directed masterpiece, "Cynthia."

As she gracefully navigated the silver screen, Elizabeth's movie star journey was just beginning, with each film propelling her closer to the zenith of Hollywood glory.

Elizabeth Taylor took off just like a lovely bird.

—*Angela Lansbury*

Pictured here is Elizabeth Taylor with her co-star Bill in a scene from *Courage of Lassie*.

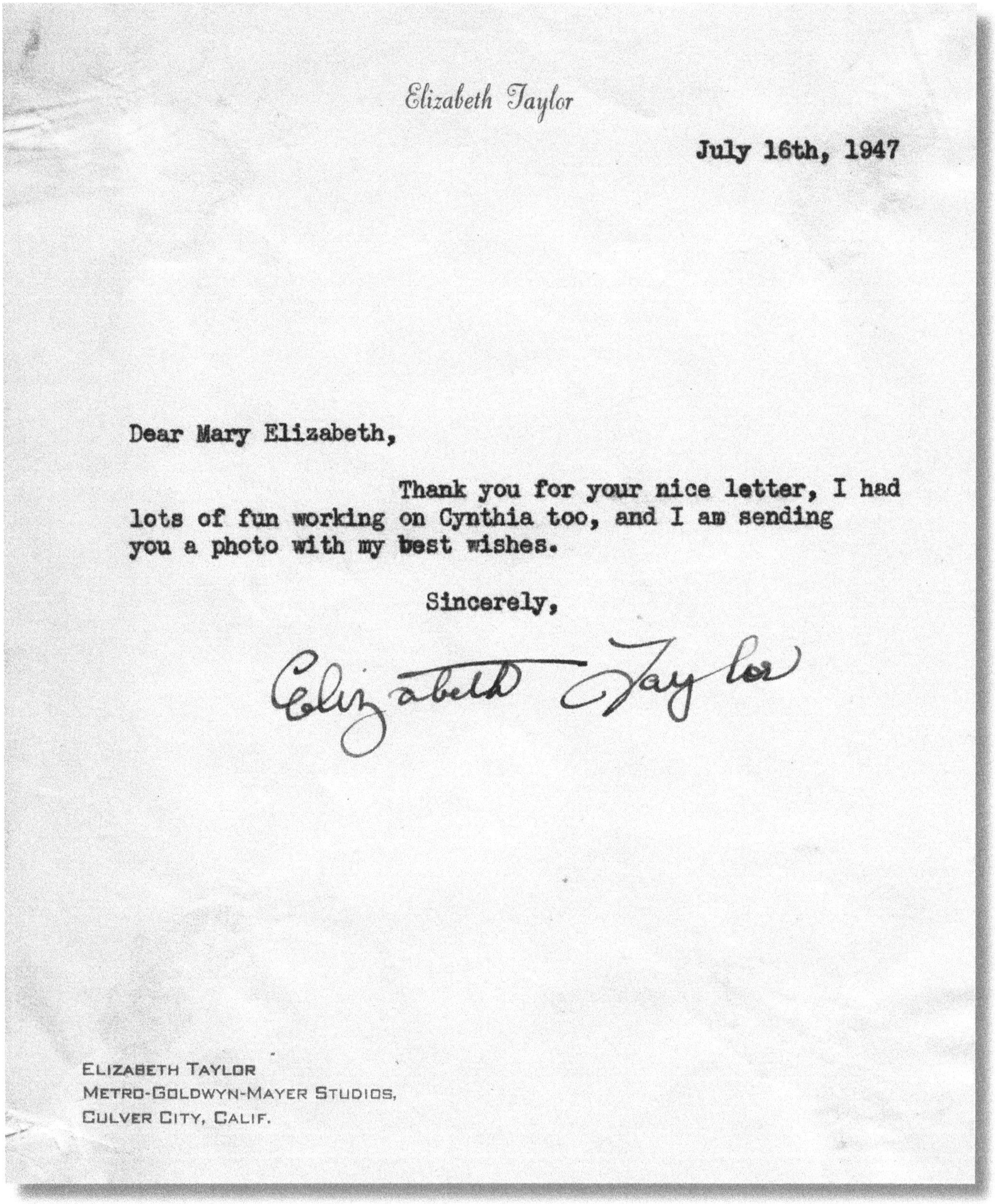

Elizabeth Taylor

July 16th, 1947

Dear Mary Elizabeth,

       Thank you for your nice letter, I had lots of fun working on Cynthia too, and I am sending you a photo with my best wishes.

       Sincerely,

       Elizabeth Taylor

ELIZABETH TAYLOR
METRO-GOLDWYN-MAYER STUDIOS,
CULVER CITY, CALIF.

In this original letter, Elizabeth talks about her work on the MGM film *Cynthia*, 1947

Source: George Houle books and autographs, Los Angeles.

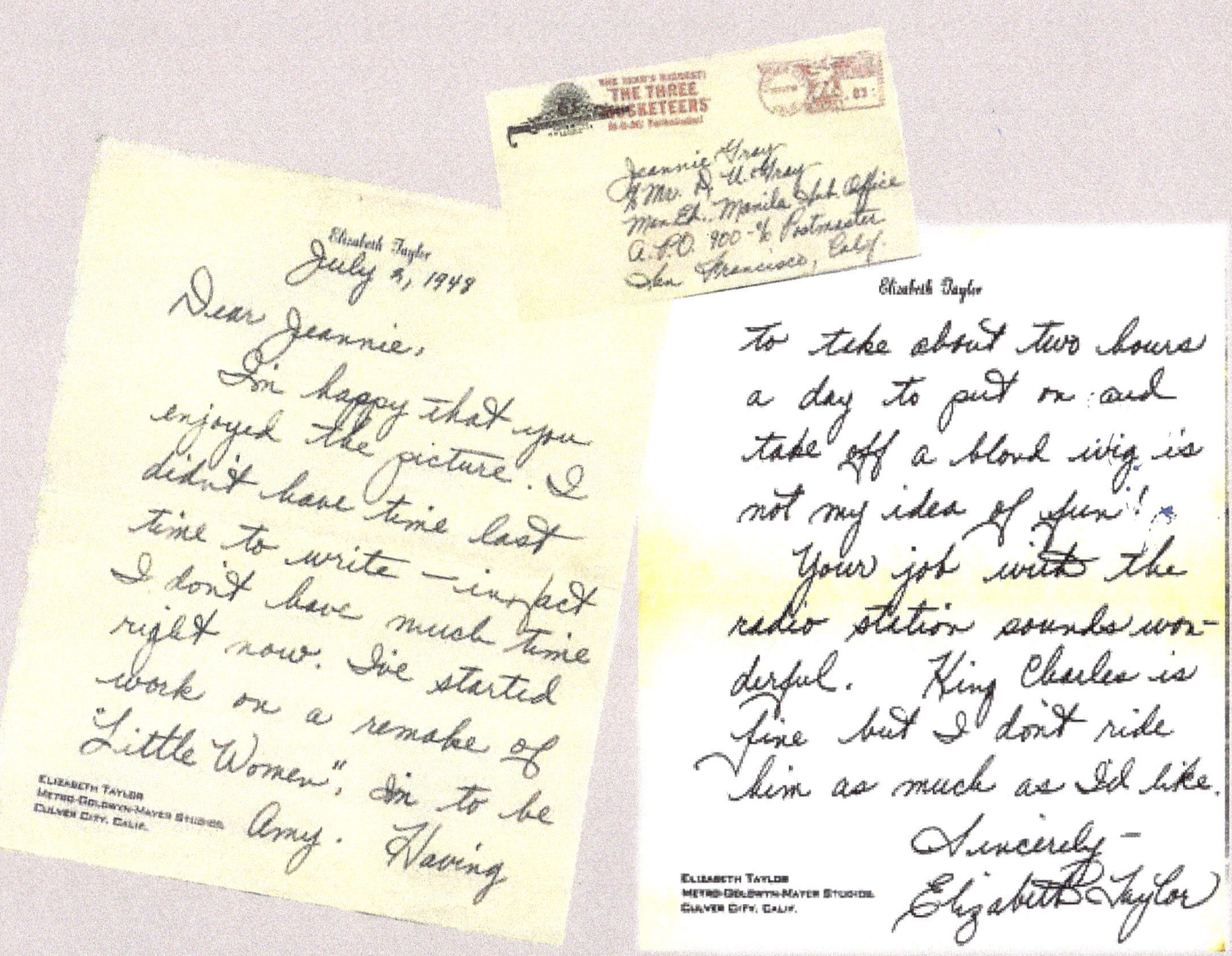

In this original handwritten letter, Elizabeth talks about King Charles, the horse MGM gave her after filming *National Velvet* and her work on her new film, *Little Women*.

It was not long before Elizabeth quickly acquired the prestigious nickname "One-Shot Liz," a reflection of her extraordinary skill and accuracy on set. With just one attempt, she effortlessly encapsulated the essence of every scene, captivating both audiences and filmmakers.

Her prowess commanded a princely sum of $2,000 per week, a testament to her rising stature in Hollywood.

As she bid farewell to her adolescent roles, Elizabeth embarked on a new chapter of her cinematic journey. Films like "A Date with Judy" (1948), "Julia Misbehaves," and the timeless 1949 classic, "Little Women," showcased her versatility and maturing talent.

While audiences may have been unprepared for Elizabeth's blossoming sensuality, the burgeoning film industry of the 1950s was ready to embrace her allure.

In 1949, Sara Taylor joined her daughter on a trip to England for Elizabeth's first adult role in "The Conspirator," where she starred alongside the charismatic Robert Taylor. It was during the filming of this movie that Elizabeth first encountered Michael Wilding, sparking a romance that would soon make headlines.

Bounded by whirlwind affairs and high-profile relationships, including a dalliance with millionaire Howard Hughes, Elizabeth's personal life became fodder for public fascination.

At the tender age of seventeen, Elizabeth encountered the harsh realities of fame, facing her first brush with fan extortion. Her captivating allure and turbulent personal life graced the front page of the Los Angeles Examiner on November 20, 1949, igniting a frenzy of media attention that would endure throughout her lifetime.

Thus began the saga of Elizabeth Taylor—a cinematic icon whose allure and mystique would captivate generations.

A STROLL DOWN THE MAIN STREET OF LONDON

This patchwork clutch is made up of small squares of animal hide. Elizabeth is pictured wearing the clutch as she and her mother stroll down the main street in London (1947). Elizabeth had gifted the clutch to her childhood friend, Ruth Culverhouse.

When Elizabeth returned from her tour of England, she was radiant. "I want a man who will understand me, one who will be there when I need him, one I can lean on. He must be the sort of man I can trust and be able to relax and certainly he must have a sense of humour." Elizabeth's childhood friend remembered how she would talk and knew she was taking about Michael Wilding.

Elizabeth Taylor: My Celebrity Connection | 43

TOUCHING UP HER MAKEUP

This miniature Helena Rubinstein lipstick is enclosed in a gold rippled casing. It was found inside the animal patch bag Elizabeth Taylor used during a trip to England with her mother. It is believed that she used it to touch up her makeup on and off the movie set. The lipstick measures 2 1/4 inches in length and 5/8-inch diameter with a twist mechanism that still works.

Source: Ruth Culverhouse estate, Bryan Hamilton son of Ruth Culverhouse and Helena Rubinstein.

44 | *Elizabeth Taylor: My Celebrity Connection*

There are no ugly women, only lazy ones.
—*Helena Rubinstein*

Elizabeth Taylor: My Celebrity Connection | 45

AUTOGRAPH-SEEKING FANS

Now that Elizabeth had become a household name, she would be stopped in the street by autograph-seeking fans. Some of Elizabeth's very first hand-signed autographs were done in mechanical pencil. This is one of the pencils Elizabeth would carry with her when meeting fans of her work.

Source: Roni Howard, personal assistant to Elizabeth from 1947 to 1971/Lisa Jones.

ANTIQUE GIFT

This is a double-stranded faux-white-pearl necklace with 24-carat-gold accents. The beads are oblong in shape. The necklace measures 14 inches in diameter. An item originally gifted from Elizabeth to a makeup artist to the stars, Ben Nye.

Elizabeth Taylor: My Celebrity Connection

MOTHER AND I

This is an original handwritten letter from Elizabeth to friend Jeannie talking about her new film and trip with her mother to England (1947).

Source: George Houle books and autographs, New York.

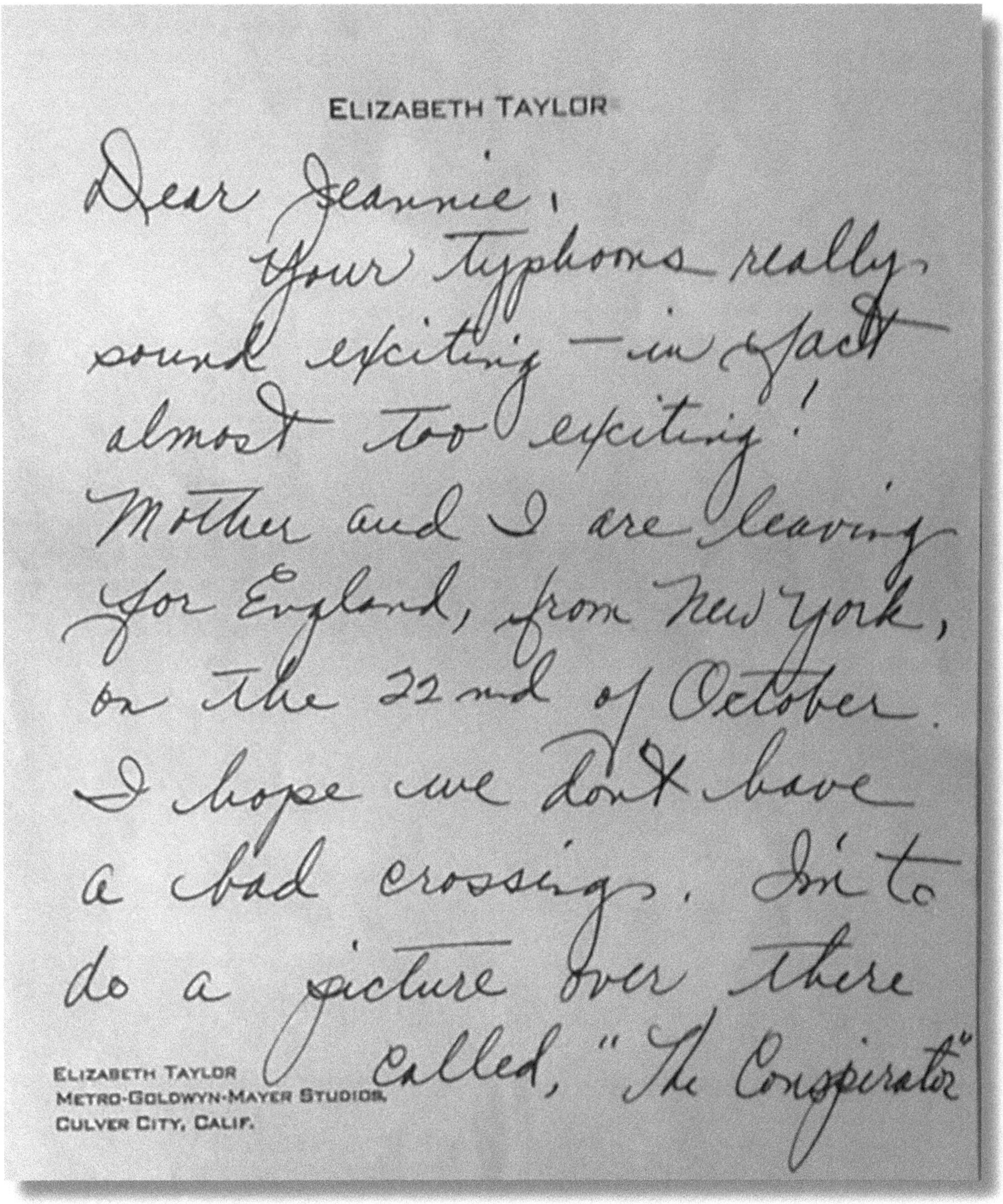

> **ELIZABETH TAYLOR**
>
> Dear Jeannie,
> Your typhoons really sound exciting — in fact almost too exciting! Mother and I are leaving for England, from New York, on the 22nd of October. I hope we don't have a bad crossing. I'm to do a picture over there called, "The Conspirator"
>
> ELIZABETH TAYLOR
> METRO-GOLDWYN-MAYER STUDIOS
> CULVER CITY, CALIF.

Elizabeth Taylor: My Celebrity Connection

BEAUTY REGIME

This porcelain rose hair clip was once part of Elizabeth's hair-and-beauty regimen. It is a hand-painted hairclip with rose petals and light-green rose leaves. The clip is 1.5 inches in diameter.

Source: Roni Howard, MGM pay clerk and personal assistant (1947-1975) to Elizabeth Taylor. Made by Shelley of England.

ROSE PETALS AND GREEN LEAVES

This porcelain hairclip dish is hand-painted with rose petals and light-green rose leaves. The dish is 3.45 inches in diameter.

Source: Roni Howard, MGM pay clerk and personal assistant (1947-1975) to Elizabeth Taylor. Made by Shelley of England.

FRANCIS TAYLOR GALLERIES

TEL. CRESTVIEW 6-4795

LONDON   BEVERLY HILLS HOTEL, SUNSET BOULEVARD   NEW YORK
BEVERLY HILLS, CALIFORNIA

June 16, 1949

Dear Sir;

    Elizabeth is away in Florida, however she may be home by the time your boys arrive here, if she has any time available I am sure she will be pleased to meet them and I suggest you telephone me when you arrive.

    This may not reach you in time but your letter of June 3 rd. addressed to the studio reached us only this morning

    Yours sincerely,

Howard Taylor

Mr. Chet Sampson
588 Lakeland
Grosse Pointe 30,
Michigan

Elizabeth's brother Howard sends correspondence on her behalf using Francis Taylor letter head paper, (June 14, 1947).

Source: George Houle books and autographs, Los Angeles.

Elizabeth was now seen as a marketable asset, and to coincide with the release of the MGM classic *Little Women*, the studio put Elizabeth's face to a new line of women's hats.

Source: *Moviegoer* magazine (1949).

Elizabeth Taylor: My Celebrity Connection | 53

Original Elizabeth autograph (1949).

54 | *Elizabeth Taylor: My Celebrity Connection*

January 26, 1950, marked a momentous evening as Elizabeth, on the cusp of her eighteenth birthday, proudly received her diploma from University High School in West Los Angeles. The air buzzed with anticipation as Elizabeth stepped into adulthood with grace and determination.

As the year unfolded, destiny wove its intricate tapestry, leading Elizabeth to the threshold of a new chapter in her life. On May 6, 1950, amid the splendour of the Good Shepherd church in Beverly Hills, Elizabeth exchanged vows with Nicholas Hilton, scion of the illustrious Waldorf-Astoria Hotel in New York and the sprawling Stevens Hotel in Chicago.

The union of two prestigious families heralded a union of opulence and promise.

However, behind the facade of marital bliss, the wedding day was a flurry of frenzied activity. In the midst of bustling preparations, Sara Taylor, Elizabeth's mother, held worries about her daughter's future.

Fearful of any obstacle hindering Elizabeth's burgeoning career, Sara took clandestine measures to ensure her daughter's reproductive health. With discreet resolve, she arranged for Elizabeth to receive a diaphragm, adamant that her daughter prioritise her professional aspirations over motherhood.

As the vows were exchanged and well-wishes abounded, a clash of desires simmered beneath the surface. While Nicholas yearned to start a family, Sara steadfastly opposed the notion, fearing it would impede Elizabeth's trajectory to success.

Newlyweds Elizabeth and Nicky Hilton are pictured here greeting guests before their departure.

Elizabeth Taylor: My Celebrity Connection

In the surrounds of this chaotic convergence of love, ambition, and familial expectations, Elizabeth Taylor stood poised, a symbol of resilience and determination in the face of uncertainty. Her journey into matrimony marked the dawn of a new era, brimming with promise and the prospect of untold adventures.

Despite the whirlwind of anticipation and preparations, Elizabeth's wedding unfolded seamlessly, much to everyone's relief. Each day brought a cascade of gifts—hats, dresses, and countless tokens of affection—eagerly received by the bride-to-be.

At intervals and during the flurry of excitement, Elizabeth's dear friend Ruth, was a steadfast source of support, ensuring that Elizabeth's special day would be nothing short of magical.

As Ruth busied herself with organising the gifts, she stumbled upon a particularly intriguing treasure—a "honeymoon nightie" crafted by none other than MGM designer, Edith Head.

Designed to allure and tantalise, this exquisite garment perfectly complemented Elizabeth's allure, with its playful peek-a-boo rear adding a cheeky touch to the ensemble.

Indeed, to describe it as merely "sexy" would be an understatement of epic proportions.

Elizabeth's penchant for alluring attire was no secret, much to the chagrin of her ever-watchful mother, who was forever engaged in a futile battle to keep her daughter's dresses from slipping too low.

Even George, the jovial chauffeur, couldn't resist a chuckle at the sight of Elizabeth's famously ample cleavage gracing the pages of magazines. "Looks like she's got a feast to accompany her main course," he would quip with a hearty laugh.

The wedding festivities, abuzz with excitement and glamour, provided a spectacular platform for MGM to showcase its latest cinematic offering, the Vincente Minnelli film "Father of the Bride," released just two days after the ceremony.

Among the attendees, actress Jane Powell stood as Elizabeth's radiant bridesmaid, adding to the allure of the occasion. Indeed, the union of Elizabeth and Nicky was a spectacle of opulence and grandeur, cementing its place as the wedding event of the century.

Pictured is Ruth Culverhouse at the age of fifteen.

When you give your daughter away in marriage, you can't possibly give all those memories along with her. Elizabeth no longer looked like a child as she and Nick knelt together. Her face had a new dignity that I'd never seen before.

—*Francis Taylor (1950)*

THE HILTONS

This sterling-silver presentation tray was gifted to Elizabeth and Conrad Hilton Jr. as a wedding gift from the former governor of Florida (1949–1953). The tray is inscribed with "The Hiltons from Gov. and Mrs. Fuller Warren." The verso is stamped "Fisher Sterling." The circular tray has a diameter of seven inches.

Source: Julien's Auction House, California/ Fisher Silversmiths Inc.

Pictured is newlywed Elizabeth Taylor Hilton with her first husband, Nicky (1950).

Source: Virginia, USA.

*There is no sure way of getting
the perfect husband—just luck, I guess.
—Elizabeth Taylor*

FROM THE CORRIDORS OF MGM

This is an original and authentic hand-coloured portrait of Elizabeth promoting the film *A Place in the Sun* (1951). The portrait originated from the corridors of MGM studios California. The portrait hung in the corridors of the MGM Studios, California. At an MGM auction in the 1970s, it was purchased by an antique dealer. In 1992, Hunter Gatherer Antiques sold the portrait to the collector.

Source: MGM Studios/ Hunter Gatherer.

The intricate details of Elizabeth's wedding gown, meticulously crafted by fifteen skilled seamstresses at MGM, were nothing short of a marvel.

Over the span of two months, they painstakingly stitched together a garment fit for a princess. Yet, despite the opulent display, the truth emerged after their honeymoon aboard the majestic Queen Mary—it seemed that a grave error had been made.

The fairy tale took a somber turn as reports surfaced of Nicky Hilton's volatile temper and struggles with alcohol. The once-promising union crumbled under the weight of irreconcilable differences, culminating in their divorce on February 1, 1951.

Despite the heartache, Elizabeth persevered, her resolve unshaken by the tumultuous end to her marriage.

Putting the personal upheaval aside, Elizabeth's career soared to new heights. She graced the silver screen once more in the sequel to "Father of the Bride," titled "Father's Little Dividend," a resounding success for the studio.

It wasn't until her collaboration with Paramount Pictures in the George Stevens classic "A Place in the Sun" that she truly captured the hearts and minds of movie goers worldwide.

Here Elizabeth signs, Elizabeth Taylor Hilton.

Set against the backdrop of George Stevens' masterful direction, "A Place in the Sun" emerged as a timeless masterpiece—a black-and-white symphony of passion and tragedy.

For Elizabeth, the role was more than just another film—it was a canvas upon which she painted her soul, delivering a performance hailed as one of her finest.

*We were just too young.
But you don't know or
realise it at the time.
A few weeks after the wedding
we both discovered
we only liked each other,
but we had stars in our eyes
and believed love would come.
—Elizabeth Taylor*

ON BOARD THE QUEEN MARY

These white cotton gloves originated from the private collection of Sydney Guilaroff. Elizabeth gave Sydney many items from her personal wardrobe over the years that they worked together. These gloves may have well been worn by Elizabeth while on board the *Queen Mary*.

Source: Sydney Guilaroff estate.

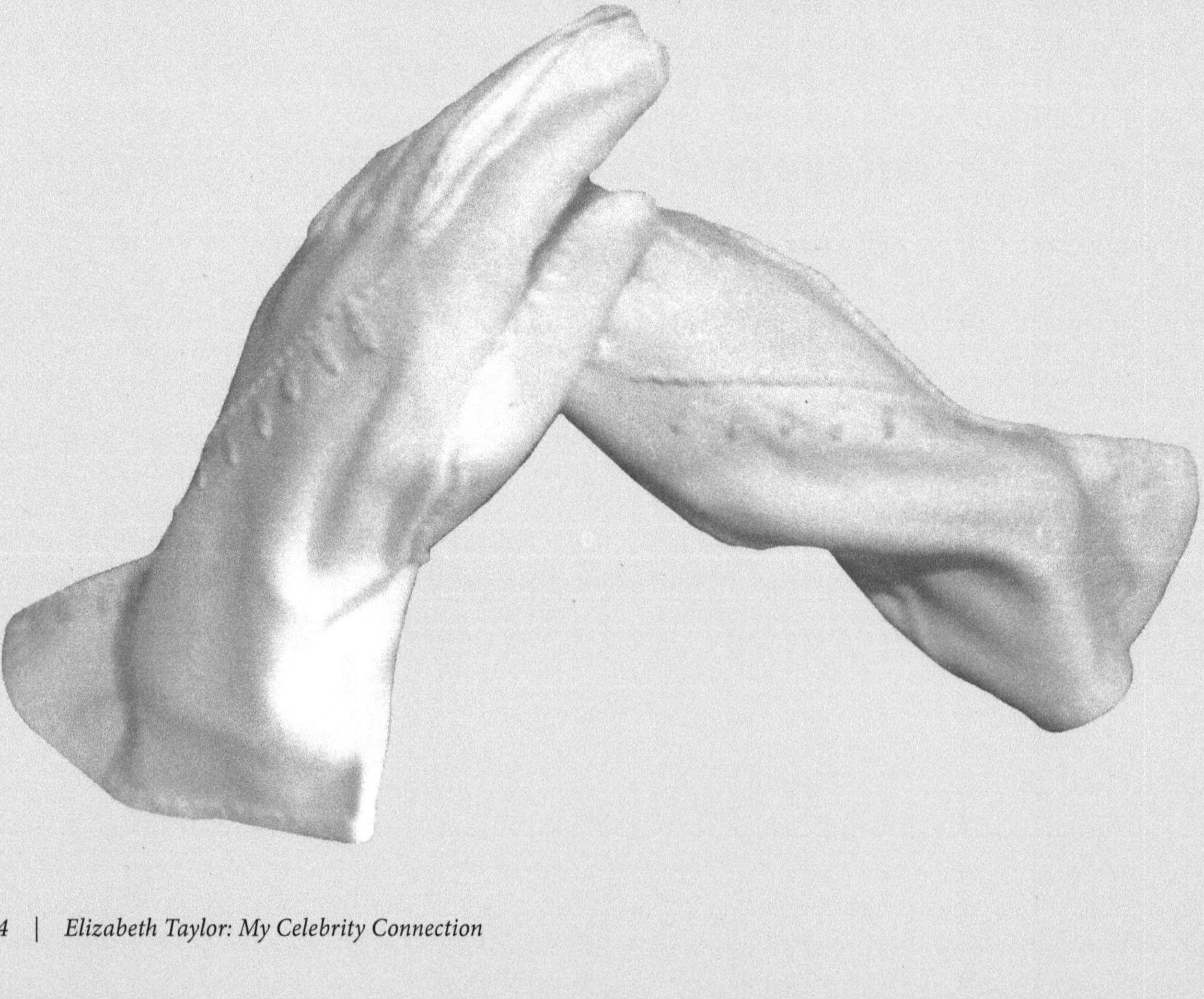

A LOVE AFFAIR WITH JEWELS

Costume jewelry was the beginning of Elizabeth Taylor's lifelong love affair with jewels of all kinds. This 16-inch necklace is encrusted with over 140 rhinestones. It has a draped-style motif and made by Kramer of New York.

Louis Kramer, who started the company in 1943, was later joined by his brothers, Morris and Harry, as he tapped into the burgeoning costume-jewelry market.

All aspects of the business took place in New York City, so the pieces were marked "Kramer," "Kramer N.Y.," or "Kramer of New York."

Source: Originally from the personal collection of Gordon Bau. The necklace was then obtained for this collection from Roslyn Herman & Co of New York.

THE DIAMOND LOOK

This is a set of two multifaceted fashion Eisenberg brooches owned and used by Elizabeth Taylor in the early to late 1940s. The words "Eisenberg Original" were used from roughly 1935 to 1945, while just plain "Eisenberg" or "Eisenberg Ice" was used from about 1945 to 1950. The jewelry became as popular as the fashions, and by the 1930s, the company began producing high-quality jewelry using the best Austrian stones to be sold separately from the clothing.

Source: Rosyn Herman and Co of New York.

These two "Eisenberg Ice"–stamped brooches were made in the mid-1940s and are adorned with Swarovski crystals and coloured stones. Eisenberg clips and/or brooches are usually festooned with aqua, ruby, and crystal stones. Many Eisenberg pieces are abstract and vaguely organic, but others resemble kings, queens, mermaids, ballerinas, and in this instance, Hollywood royalty Dame Elizabeth Taylor.

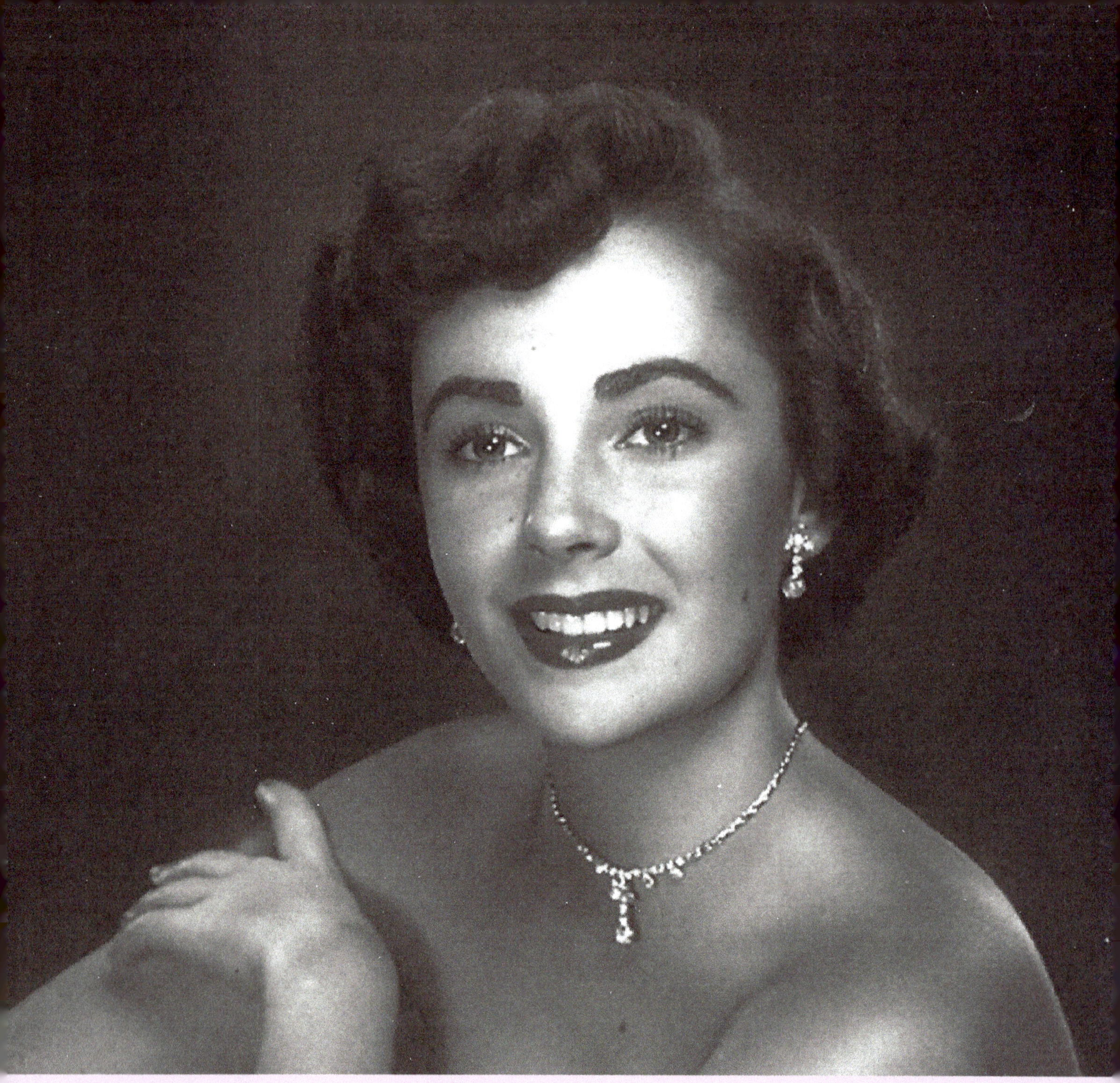

This original 1950s fashion jewelry was the beginning of Elizabeth's lifelong love affair with jewels.

68 | *Elizabeth Taylor: My Celebrity Connection*

With each passing year, Elizabeth's star ascended to even greater heights, her talent commanding an astonishing salary of over $5,500 per week.

In 1952 alone, she dazzled audiences with her captivating performances in two cinematic gems: "Love Is Better Than Ever" and Richard Thorpe's epic production of "Ivanhoe."

As the world marvelled at her on-screen prowess, Elizabeth's personal life took centre stage once more. Just days before her twentieth birthday, she embarked on a new chapter of her journey, exchanging vows with the dashing Michael Wilding in a private ceremony at Claridge's in London.

Their union bore fruit swiftly, with Elizabeth soon expecting their first child.

On January 6, 1953, the couple welcomed their son, Michael Howard Wilding, into the world—a joyous occasion marked by the endearing nicknames "Britches" and "Michael the Noise." Yet, surrounded by the joy of parenthood, clouds of concern loomed on the horizon.

Michael Wilding, ever the devoted husband and father, expressed reservations about Elizabeth's demanding film schedule. Aware of her delicate health, he advocated for a more restrained workload, mindful of her slight cardiac weakness. Little did they know that this seemingly minor ailment would later escalate into congestive heart failure, ultimately claiming Elizabeth's life.

Elizabeth Taylor: My Celebrity Connection

Elizabeth waits at the Los Angeles airport for a flight to England, signed in person (1953).

Source: Joe Decker.

Elizabeth Taylor: My Celebrity Connection | 71

HONORARY PRESIDENT

In 1953, Elizabeth was honorary president of the Elizabeth Taylor Fan Club. Fans like Marilyn Hill received a beautiful collection of images of Elizabeth and a signed membership card from Elizabeth herself.

Throughout her seventy-year career, Elizabeth always took time to correspond with her fans, including yours truly.

Source: Marilyn Hill (1953).

Elizabeth shares a scene with Fernado Lamas in the film, *The Girl Who had Everything* (1954).

Source: MGM.

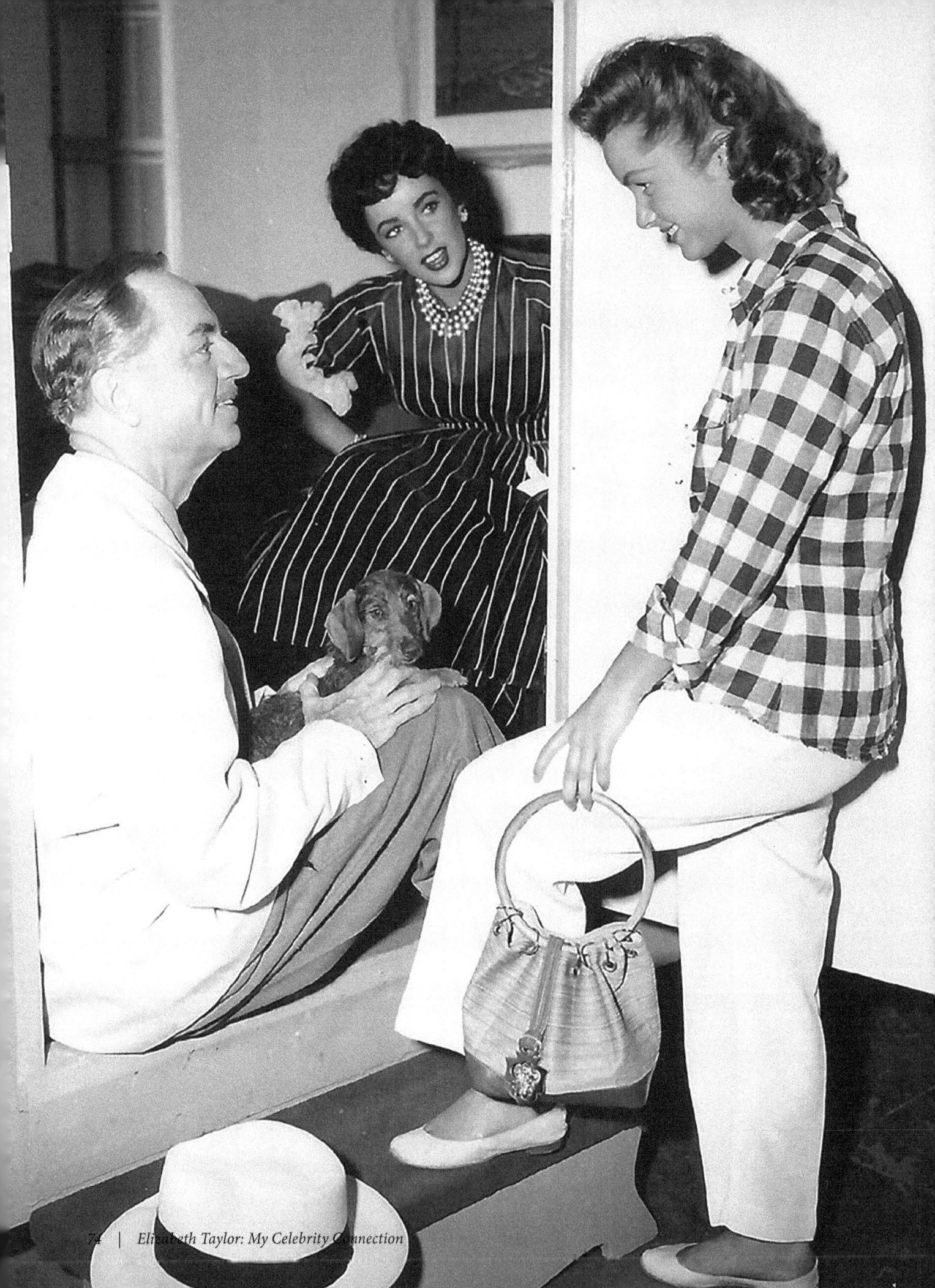

A young Debbie Reynolds visits Elizabeth and co-stars Gig Young and William Powell on the set of *The Girl Who had Everything* (1954).

Source: Clarence S. Bull estate.

Despite basking in the glow of critical acclaim, Elizabeth found herself yearning for more substantial roles as she navigated the tumultuous waters of Hollywood.

Disenchanted with the offerings presented to her, she eagerly awaited the opportunity to grace the silver screen once more.

In 1953, Elizabeth's hunger for compelling roles intensified. Her eyes turned towards "Elephant Walk," a William Dieterle film tailor-made for her talents.

However, fate had other plans. Pregnant with her second child, Christopher, Elizabeth reluctantly declined the coveted role.

In a twist of fate, Vivien Leigh, renowned for her striking resemblance to Elizabeth, stepped into the spotlight, poised to bring the character to life. Yet, the stars did not align, and the role ultimately found its way back into Elizabeth's capable hands.

A curious footnote to the film's production lies in the opening scene—a poignant reminder of the intricate dance between fate and fortune.

Is that Elizabeth or Vivien in the bookstore?

Source: MGM.

THE LAST TIME I SAW PARIS

This wig was worn by Elizabeth in her role as Helen Ellswirth in the 1954 romantic drama, "The Last Time I saw Paris".

This short brown wig is made from real human hair and includes original hairpins, storage box, and wig-stock record—an amazing piece of Hollywood history. In her role as Helen, Elizabeth got caught out in the rain and developed pneumonia and died in the film.

Source: MGM Wig Works/ MGM movie and memorabilia auction in 1974 / Heritage Auctions, Texas.

Elizabeth Taylor: My Celebrity Connection | 79

Elizabeth Taylor
Hollywood, Calif.

March 24, 1955

Dear Claire,

Thank you so much for the lovely, little pink kimona.

Both Michael and I think it is so cute, and we can't wait to see it on Christopher!

It was so very thoughtful of you to send such a nice gift, and I do appreciate your kindness.

Sincerely,

Elizabeth Taylor

ET/js

Elizabeth and Michael receive a lovely gift for newly born Christopher from a fan by the name of Claire (1955).

Source: Harmonie Collectables, USA.

Elizabeth Taylor: My Celebrity Connection | 81

In a whirlwind of activity, Elizabeth Taylor was now juggling the demands of motherhood with an insatiable hunger for more meaningful roles, completing films like "Rhapsody," "Beau Brummell," and "The Last Time I Saw Paris" within a mere twelve months, Elizabeth found herself at the precipice of exhaustion. Yet, her relentless pursuit of artistic fulfillment knew no bounds.

Against this backdrop of frenetic activity, a momentous event unfolded—the birth of Christopher Edward Wilding on February 27, 1955.

Despite the challenges she faced, Elizabeth remained undeterred, her resolve unyielding in the face of adversity.

At the tender age of twenty-three, with two children and a staggering twenty-five films to her name, Elizabeth had traversed the precipitous terrain of Hollywood with unparalleled grace and determination.

Despite her status as the epitome of beauty in America and beyond, doubts lingered regarding Elizabeth's prowess as an actor.

Critics, fans, and even Elizabeth herself grappled with the elusive notion of greatness—a quest that seemed perpetually out of reach.

However, as the years unfolded, Elizabeth Taylor's legacy transcended the silver screen. Her journey, marked by triumphs and tribulations, and epitomised by transformative power of resilience.

In Elizabeth, the world found not just a starlet, but a striking force for change and compassion—a legacy that continues to inspire generations today

In a remarkable evolution, she would emerge as a beacon of hope and compassion—an outspoken advocate for human equality and HIV-AIDS awareness.

Elizabeth entered motherhood and did not return to the silver screen until early 1956, in the film *Giant*.

Source: Culver Pictures.

Having children didn't change Elizabeth, it broadened her; she didn't get dressed up, she used to just slob around.

—*Liz Smith, columnist*

Throughout the buzz of anticipation, Elizabeth embarked on a transformative journey into the heart of Texas in the George Stevens epic, "Giant." Based on Edna Ferber's acclaimed novel, this cinematic masterpiece brought together a stellar cast, including the likes of Rock Hudson and the enigmatic James Dean.

In a tour de force performance, Elizabeth's character, Leslie Benedict, traversed the passage of time, aging over fifty years before the audience's eyes.

Her portrayal earned her a staggering $175,000, a testament to her undeniable talent and star power. Meanwhile, George Stevens' masterful direction garnered accolades, culminating in an Academy Award for his captivating portrayal of the Texan family saga.

However, tragedy was about to strike with immense impact. During the filming, the vibrant young talent, James Dean, met an untimely end in a tragic car accident. Elizabeth was left reeling from the loss of her co-star and friend, and his absence casted a shadow over the production.

James Dean reportedly spent his final moments with Elizabeth and her friends, a poignant reminder of the ephemeral nature of life.

As the news of his passing reverberated through Hollywood, Elizabeth grappled with the weight of grief, mourning the loss of a promising talent gone too soon.

In a touching snapshot captured on the set of "Giant," Elizabeth shares a moment of camaraderie with her co-stars, indulging in the simple pleasures of watermelon amidst the Texas heat.

In the middle of life's highs and lows, Elizabeth's spirit continued to shine, a beacon of resilience and grace in the face of adversity.

Elizabeth radiates with beauty in this unseen candid image. Here she is seen at the world premiere of George Stevens' production of *Giant* at the Roxy theatre, West Hollywood, a benefit for the Muscular Dystrophy Association of America (1956).

Source: Edgar Vash/Barry Taub.

Elizabeth Taylor
Hollywood, Calif.

September 9, 1955

Dear Margie,

Sorry I've been so **terribly** long in answering your letter. I really didn't think it had been that long until I looked at the date.

We've been working very hard on Giant, and I haven't been getting home 'til late. Sometimes even 11:00 at night. I guess it's pretty easy to see why I haven't been getting much done.

In answer to your questions, I imagine you can write Jane Withers at Warners, as she'll be working there a short time, yet, and I'm sure they'll forward it to her if she's not working.

Yes, I do know Peter Thompson, a very nice person to know. Sorry, but I really don't know who will be in the cast for Maryanne, I guess we'll just have to wait and be surprised.

Do forgive me for making this so brief, I have just too many things to do! Will try to make it longer next time.

Love,

In a personal note to "Margie", dated September 9, 1955, Elizabeth speaks of her work on the film "Giant" and her late filming hours.

Elizabeth Taylor and James Dean relax on the coach during a break in filming 1956.

The script cover to Giant, dated April 4, 1955, is signed by James Dean, Rock Hudson and Elizabeth Taylor.

Elizabeth's role as Leslie Benedict in *Giant* is captured in this unique celebrity doll.

Source: Franklin Mint.

Elizabeth Taylor: My Celebrity Connection | 91

Elizabeth Taylor's transformation from beloved starlet to formidable adult actor left critics and audiences alike in awe, marking the beginning of her renowned ten-year reign.

Her portrayal in "Raintree County," under the direction of Edward Dmytryk, showcased a newfound maturity and power, earning her the prestigious honour of her first Academy Award nomination and a coveted star on the Hollywood Walk of Fame.

As Elizabeth's career soared to new heights, her personal life was still fraught with turmoil. Despite her professional success, her marriage to Michael Wilding faltered, culminating in her second divorce on January 30, 1957.

In the centre of the chaos, Elizabeth found solace in the arms of Mike Todd, a seasoned figure in the world of romance.

For Elizabeth, love bloomed anew in the embrace of the charismatic Mike Todd, whose life had been marked by tragedy and triumph. Their union, sealed in a quaint Spanish civil ceremony in Puerto Marques. Surrounded by armed Mexican troops, Elizabeth and Mike exchanged vows in a spectacle shrouded in secrecy.

Mike, ever the romantic, showered his bride with tokens of his affection—a dazzling array of diamond-studded jewellery valued at a staggering $87,000.

The wedding party, including singer Eddie Fisher as best man and Debbie Reynolds as matron of honor, added to the glamour and splendour of the occasion.

As Elizabeth embarked on this new chapter of her life, the world watched in amazement, captivated by the whirlwind romance and undeniable chemistry between the violet-eyed beauty and her dashing suitor. Their love story would be remembered as a saga of passion, opulence, and enduring devotion.

RAINTREE COUNTY

Behold, a relic from the golden age of cinema—an original hoop dress meticulously crafted for the MGM classic, "Raintree County" released in 1957.

Designed by the legendary Walter Plunkett, this exquisite ensemble adorned the radiant form of Elizabeth Taylor, capturing the essence of a bygone era.

In a mesmerising scene, Elizabeth graces the screen in this very hoop dress, her presence a vision of ethereal beauty. The dress, carefully adorned with bamboo hoops and delicate lace, served as the canvas for a moment in cinematic history—a scene where Elizabeth's character confronts the shadows of her past with raw emotion.

As if infused with the spirit of its illustrious wearer, this hoop dress embarked on a remarkable journey, traversing continents and captivating audiences worldwide.

From its humble beginnings on the sets of MGM studios to its eventual acquisition by Barbara Awerkamp in the 1970s, this dress bore witness to the passage of time and the enduring legacy of Elizabeth Taylor.

Now, nestled within the confines of "Elizabeth Taylor My Celebrity Connection," this cherished artifact finds its rightful place—a testament to the timeless allure of Hollywood's golden age.

For Angela Schneider at Tinsel and Stars, the journey of this dress culminates in a moment of bittersweet serenity, knowing that its final resting place is among the treasures of the lifestyle that was Elizabeth Taylor.

Source: Angela Schneider at Tinsel and Stars, Los Angeles, California. It was purchased from Angela in 2017 for this collection.

THE RAINTREE COUNTY PICNIC

Marvel at the tales woven into the fabric of this humble picnic basket, a vessel brimming with memories from the celebrated film set of "Raintree County".

Picture it: shared moments of respite amid the hustle and bustle, where cast and crew came together to partake in simple joys. Feast your eyes on delicate handkerchiefs adorned with horse heads, antique German dessert plates gleaming with gold trim, and a set of exquisite mother-of-pearl-handled knives cradled in a felt roll tie.

And behold, nestled among them, the gleaming silver salt and pepper shakers crafted by none other than the esteemed Wilcox International Silver Co.

But the wonders don't end there. A quilt, lovingly crafted by Barbara's mother during the turmoil of World War II, serves as both a symbol of comfort and a practical picnic blanket for the stars of "Raintree County." Its light blue hues and intricate Jacob's ladder pattern bear witness to years of cherished use.

As Barbara Burgin Leigh's daughter, Jamie, recounts, these items were more than mere props—they were conduits of camaraderie, shared laughter, and fleeting moments of respite. And amidst it all, Montgomery Clift, still recovering from his recent ordeal, found solace in the company of friends.

Even decades later, the echoes of laughter and camaraderie linger, as recalled by the luminous Eva Marie Saint, a testament to the enduring magic of Hollywood's golden age.

Source: Jamie Leigh. Item purchased for this collection before an estate sale in 2013.

ELIZABETH WAS VERY GIVING

Behold the exquisite token of generosity bestowed by the luminous Elizabeth Taylor—a delicate and enchanting Ernst and Carl Eduard Bucherer Swiss pendant watch, adorned with 24-carat gold and suspended from a graceful 32-inch chain.

Image Elizabeth, adorned with this timeless treasure, as she graced the idyllic landscapes of Central Kentucky during the filming of "Raintree County."

But this watch holds more than mere beauty—it carries with it the spirit of friendship. Elizabeth, ever gracious, gifted this precious keepsake to Thelma, a dear friend of Barbara Brandt Burgin Leigh.

Together, Barbara and Thelma would prepare picnic baskets for their riverside rendezvous on the tranquil banks of the Dix River in Lincoln County.

And on those special occasions, Elizabeth would join them, her presence infusing each moment with an undeniable charm.

Take a closer look at the intricate details of this timepiece—the 2.5-centimeter diameter case adorned with an enchanting enamel motif of pink and green florals and leaves. Each link of the chain, approximately half an inch in length, intricately joined together to form a seamless connection.

As the hands of time continued their eternal dance, this cherished heirloom found its way into the hands of Jamie Leigh, daughter of Barbara Brandt Burgin Leigh. In 2013, Jamie, recognising the significance of this piece of Hollywood history, entrusted it to the collection, ensuring that its legacy would endure for generations to come.

Source: Jamie Leigh. Item purchased for this collection before an estate sale in 2013.

These are captivating snapshots from the enchanting world of "Raintree County"! Here, in one frame, we witness the youthful exuberance of little James "Jim" Burgin Leigh alongside his uncle, Welby Burgin, as they frolic on the train set—a timeless relic from another era.

Can you believe that this majestic locomotive, a century-old marvel, journeyed across the country on its very own flat car, transported all the way from the Baltimore museum to grace the silver screen?

And there, in another captivating image, we catch a glimpse of Barbara "Bob" Brandt Burgin Leigh, resplendent in her nurse uniform.

Little did she know that nestled within the confines of her mother's bank safe at the Lincoln County National Bank lay a precious treasure—a pendant that once adorned the graceful neck of none other than Elizabeth Taylor herself!

AN EMBELLISHED BRACELET

This bracelet is 10 centimetres in diameter and is structured with small embellished silver panels that link together with eight silver leaves-like links. It has a sterling-silver safety chain that ensures a secure fit.

Source: Jamie Leigh.

BEAUMONT INN HARRODSBURG

Step into the mesmerising tale of Beaumont Inn in Harrodsburg, where enchantment and history intertwine!

This captivating ensemble—a beautiful blue velvet hat, a delicate hat box, a regal 17-inch princess string of pearls, a foldaway ashtray, and elegant hat pins—has been safeguarded by Edward Parkes since they were first bestowed upon his beloved wife, Sallie, by none other than Elizabeth Taylor herself.

Picture this: in the year 1956, Edward Parkes and his soon-to-be wife, Sallie, found themselves dining at the illustrious Beaumont Inn in Kentucky. As they savoured their meal, Edward's eyes fell upon a familiar figure across the room—an old comrade from his World War II days.

To Sallie's incredulity, Edward revealed that the man was none other than the renowned actor Lee Marvin, who happened to be in the vicinity for the filming of "Raintree County."

With a mix of disbelief and curiosity, Sallie questioned the authenticity of Edward's claim. Undeterred, Edward seized the moment, taking Sallie by the hand and leading her straight to Lee Marvin's table. And thus began a chance encounter that would leave an indelible mark on their lives—a meeting that would culminate in a precious gift from Elizabeth Taylor herself.

Elizabeth Taylor: My Celebrity Connection

The enchanting tale continues! The very next week, Edward and Sallie embarked on a remarkable journey to the film set, guided by none other than Lee Marvin himself, who warmly introduced his wartime companion to the illustrious cast. Sallie, with her innate elegance and grace, found herself captivated by the entire spectacle.

As filming unfolded, they found themselves frequent visitors to the set, basking in the magic of the cinematic world. But the wonders didn't end there! They were graciously welcomed into the inner circle of the cast, invited to exclusive dinner soirées as honoured guests of Lee Marvin himself.

In those intimate gatherings, they forged lasting bonds with the talented ensemble, sharing laughter, stories, and unforgettable moments that would forever be etched in their hearts.

Elizabeth Taylor: My Celebrity Connection | 101

According to Edward, Ms. Taylor seemed to sense Sallie's admiration, and as filming drew to a close, she bestowed upon Sallie some exquisite keepsakes—a stunning boxed navy velvet hat adorned with pearls, accompanied by a string of elegant princess pearls.

The captivating tale of "Raintree County" and its cherished artifacts first came to light through a serendipitous encounter with Jamie, daughter of Barbara Brandt Leigh. Jamie, in her generosity, passed on her mother's cherished "Raintree County" story and artifacts to this remarkable collection.

And the thread of providence intertwines further: it is said that Jamie's husband once cared for Mrs. Sallie Parkes, leading to their initial acquaintance.

Through the passage of time and the eventual passing of Mrs. Sallie Parkes, Jamie and her husband maintained a meaningful connection with Edward Parkes, culminating in the fascinating journey of these extraordinary items.

In the enchanting era of her marriage to Mike Todd, Elizabeth's life took a remarkable turn, transforming her from the "poor little rich girl" to a woman who seemingly had it all. On August 6, 1957, Elizabeth welcomed her first daughter, Elizabeth Frances Todd, affectionately known as Liza, into the world through a momentous caesarean section.

Mike Todd played a pivotal role in Elizabeth's liberation, freeing her from the clutches of control and dominance that had long defined her relationship with her mother and the MGM studio system.

With Todd by her side, Elizabeth embarked on a journey into a realm of boundless freedom and exhilaration, leaving behind the constraints of her past to embrace a future brimming with possibility and excitement.

Mike Todd is embraced by his wife while he reflects on his life after winning an Academy Award for his film, *Around the World in 80 Days*, which grossed over $17 million at the box office.

Elizabeth Taylor: My Celebrity Connection

I've fallen in love for the first time.
—Elizabeth Taylor

When receiving the award, Mike said, "I can't believe it, to win two of the biggest prizes in one year, the Academy Award and my darling wife, Elizabeth. I must be the luckiest man alive."
—Mike Todd

ELIZABETH TOURS AUSTRALIA

Embarking on a whirlwind journey to promote "Around the World in 80 Days," the Todds set foot in Melbourne, Australia, on November 7, 1957, following a gruelling twenty-six-hour flight.

Their arrival at the Menzies Hotel sparked a frenzy among over eight hundred eager fans, who clamoured for a glimpse of the beloved couple.

The ensuing day witnessed a remarkable gesture as Mike Todd and the illustrious film-star, Elizabeth, presented a staggering cheque of 14,171 pounds to the esteemed Lord Mayor Cr Thomas at the town hall, leaving an indelible mark of generosity on the city.

Before their departure several days later, a devoted fan named Peter Tremayne bestowed upon Elizabeth a remarkable three-foot, six-inch kangaroo crafted from genuine kangaroo skin.

Captured in timeless images are the Todds, exuding elegance and grace, at Ascot in Sydney, Australia, in 1957, amidst an atmosphere of adoration and excitement.

Source: Unknown, candid snapshot of Elizabeth when on tour in Australia in 1957.

Elizabeth and husband Mike Todd attended the Regent Theatre, Melbourne, Australia.

Source: Philip Hartley.

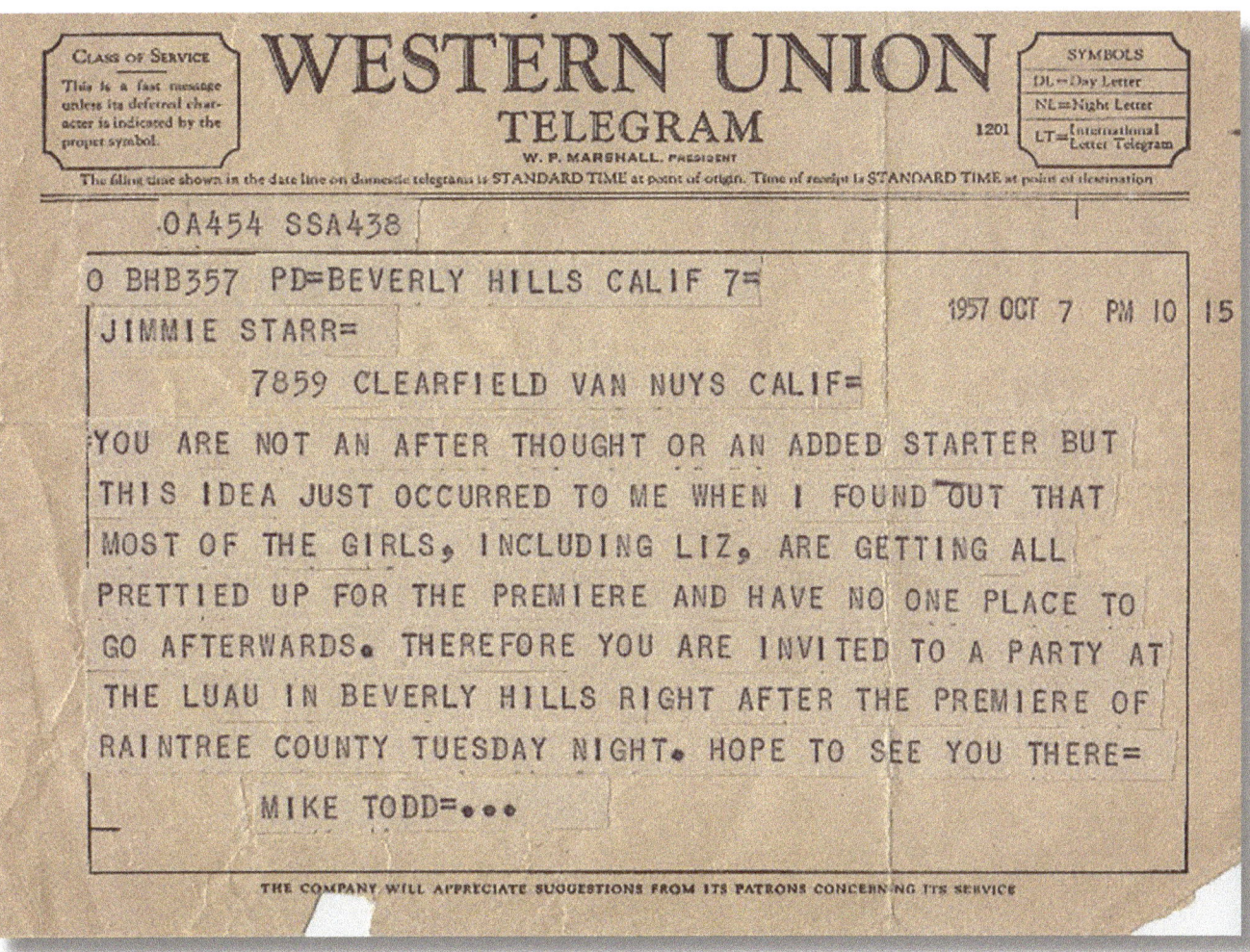

In a Western Union telegram dated, October 7, 1957, Mike Todd sends an invite to Jimmie Star, inviting him to attend a party that is to be held at the Luan, Beverly Hills right after the premiere of Raintree Country.

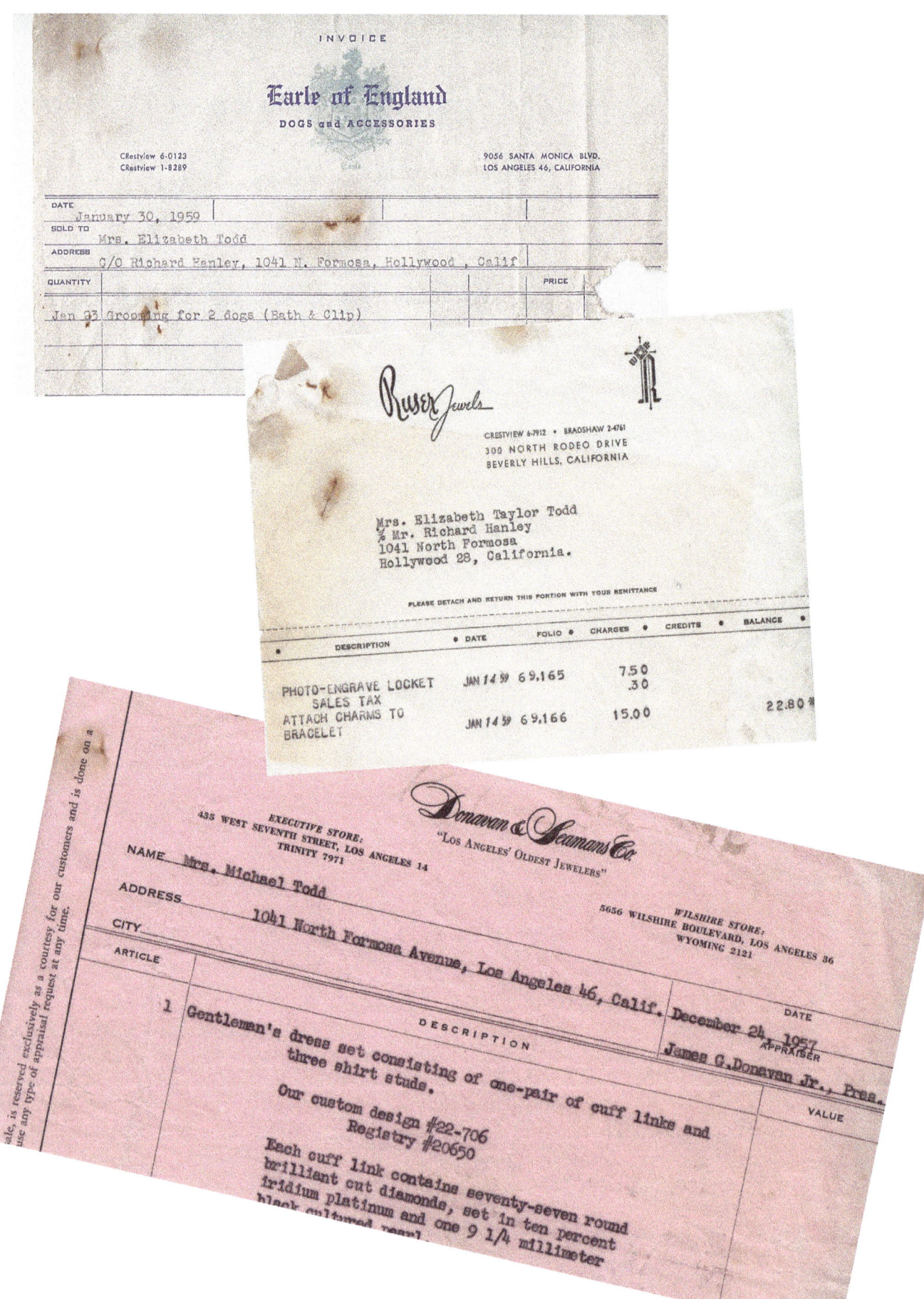

110 | *Elizabeth Taylor: My Celebrity Connection*

DOUBLE-BREASTED HERRINGBONE COAT

This blended woolen coat was owned and worn by Elizabeth in the late 1950s. This is a cream-silk-wool-blend double-breasted coat with a herringbone weave and pearlized buttons. The label reads "dejue Paris."

Elizabeth is pictured wearing a similar-styled coat that helps create a good comparison to the one described.

Source: Julien's Celebrity Auctions in Beverly Hills/ Michael and Fredericka Lam, the founders of the Great American Doll Company.

Elizabeth Taylor: My Celebrity Connection | 111

In a heart-wrenching tragedy on the night of March 21, 1958, the twin-engine Lockheed Lodestar, christened the "Liz," ascended to over 1,300 feet, only to plummet moments later over the majestic Zuñi mountains of New Mexico.

The crash claimed the lives of Mike Todd (50), his esteemed biographer, Art Cohen (49), and seasoned pilots William Verner (45) and Tom Barclay (34), extinguishing their vibrant spirits in an instant.

Amidst the devastation, on Tuesday, March 25, 1958, Elizabeth, escorted by her brother, Howard Taylor, and her physician, Dr. Frexford Kennemer, arrived at the graveside. Overwhelmed by grief, Elizabeth broke free from her escorts and threw herself onto her husband's final resting place, her anguished sobs echoing through the somber air.

Although the Jewish service at Walheim Cemetery forbade eulogies, Michael Todd Jr. (29) delivered a poignant and heartfelt tribute to his late father, offering solace in the midst of profound loss.

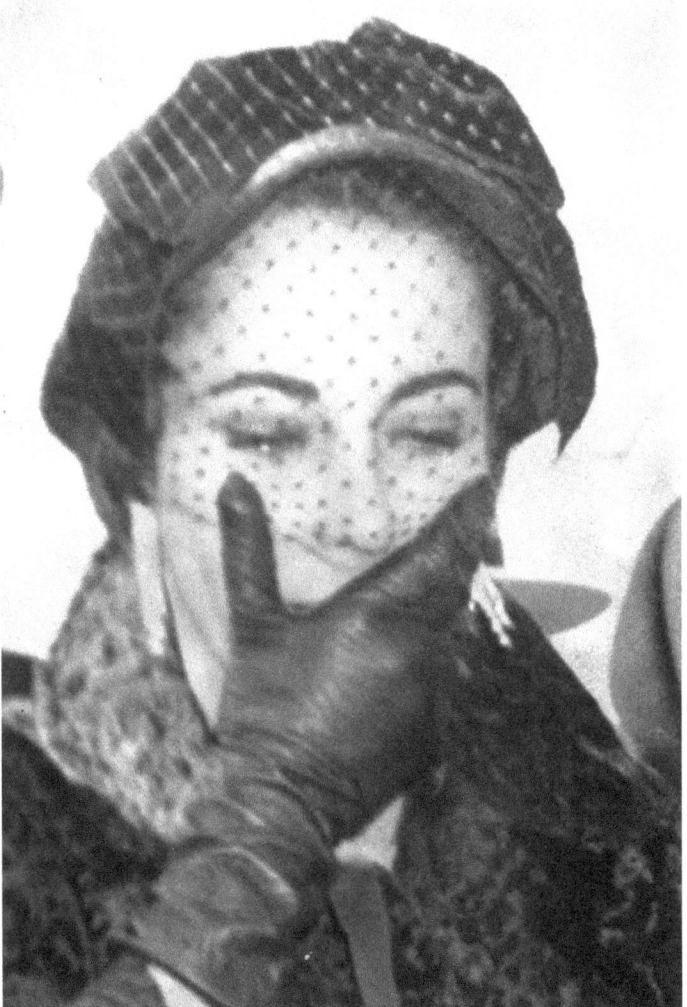

Elizabeth Todd responds to a letter of condolence regarding the loss of husband, Mike Todd.

Elizabeth sheds a tear as she leaves Mike Todd's gravesite (1958).

Source: United Press International.

A CRYSTAL PIN BROOCH

This elegant lime-green Austrian Swarovski crystal pin brooch was made in Australia and purchased for Elizabeth by her then-husband Mike Todd when she made a one-time visit promoting Todd's film *Around the World in 80 Days* in 1957.

Source: Sourced from Disneyland Parks and Resorts, Florida.

In the wake of Mike's tragic departure, Elizabeth, seeking solace received counsel from her physician, Dr. Rex Kennamer, to rid herself of any mementos gifted by Mike.

With a heavy heart, Elizabeth instructed her trusted personal assistant, Roni Howard, to clear out her storage space.

Remarkably, she granted Roni permission to keep any items he desired, a gesture underscoring her generosity even in the depths of her grief.

Lipstick No 2

Tussy Cosmetics "Contraband" is etched on fleur-de-lis case. The lipstick is contained in a 24-carat-gold-plated case (ca 1947).

Source: Lisa Maalouf/ Roni Howard estate.

ELIZABETH'S HEAD WRAP

This is a pale-blue head wrap/dress with circular fabric panels throughout, which is open at the back and is tied off with two blue ribbons. It appears to have been custom-made as it has no size and/or label.

Source: Roni Howard estate, personal assistant to Elizabeth Taylor from 1947 to 1972.

Schwab's Pharmacy prescriptions made out to Elizabeth Todd (Mrs Todd) and prescribed by her then physician, Dr. Frexford Kennemer.

THE TAYLOR-TODD ESTATE

This handcrafted gold hairbrush is believed to have been gifted to Elizabeth by her mother, Sara, in the late 1940s. It became one of the many items that personal assistant to Elizabeth, Roni Howard, saved when asked to clean out a storage area at the Taylor-Todd estate.

Source: Lisa Maalouf/ Roni Howard estate.

THE HAIR BRUSH SET

This hairbrush set was another item saved from the storage clean out.

Source: Lisa Maalouf/ Roni Howard estate.

ELIZABETH'S CURLY LOCKS

These are an assortment of curlers and pins used to beautify Elizabeth's beautiful locks.

Strands of Elizabeth's hair are still attached to many of the curlers.

Source: Lisa Maalouf/ Roni Howard estate.

THE CLEAR CRYSTAL PERFUME BOTTLE

This clear crystal bottle was given to Elizabeth from then-husband Mike Todd.

Source: Lisa Maalouf/ Roni Howard estate.

Following Mike Todd's tragic departure, Elizabeth experienced a newfound sense of liberation, igniting her portrayal of Maggie the Cat in the compelling film "Cat on a Hot Tin Roof," a performance that earned her a remarkable second Academy Award nomination.

Struggle with the lingering memories of her late husband, Elizabeth sought solace in the arms of Eddie Fisher, then-husband of Debbie Reynolds. A mere seven months after Mike Todd's passing, Elizabeth exchanged vows with Eddie Fisher (Edwin John Fisher) on May 12, 1959.

In a stunning green wedding dress, Elizabeth made a memorable entrance, arriving eighteen minutes late for the fifteen-minute sundown ceremony, held at the Beth Shalom Jewish temple in Los Angeles. It was during this time that Elizabeth embraced Judaism, marking the climax of Hollywood's most sensational love triangle.

Debbie Reynolds is captured here offering solace to her dear friend Elizabeth Taylor (1958).

Source: Mexico/Daily New, Australia.

At the time of Mike Todd's death, they were both residing at 1330 Schuyder Drive, Beverly Hills, California. This picture was taken the day of Mike Todd's death. This is the house where Elizabeth's payroll assistant was instructed to clear out unwanted items stored in the garage of the property.

LULU BRIDAL WEAR

This item is believed to have come from the estate of Eddie Fisher. It is labelled "Lula." Lula is one of the world's leading brands of bridal and evening wear. This Wedding gown is made of satin. The neckline and shoulders are embellished with floral-patterned lace and small pearl buttons. The sleeves are also embellished with a quarter-length lace and button up on the sides with several pearl buttons.

Whilst this is not the gown Elizabeth wore during her wedding to her third husband, Eddie Fisher, it could be assumed that it was one that was considered at the time and put to the side, given that it was in the possession of the Eddie Fisher estate when he passed away in September of 2010.

Source: Celebrity Seconds/ Eddie Fisher estate.

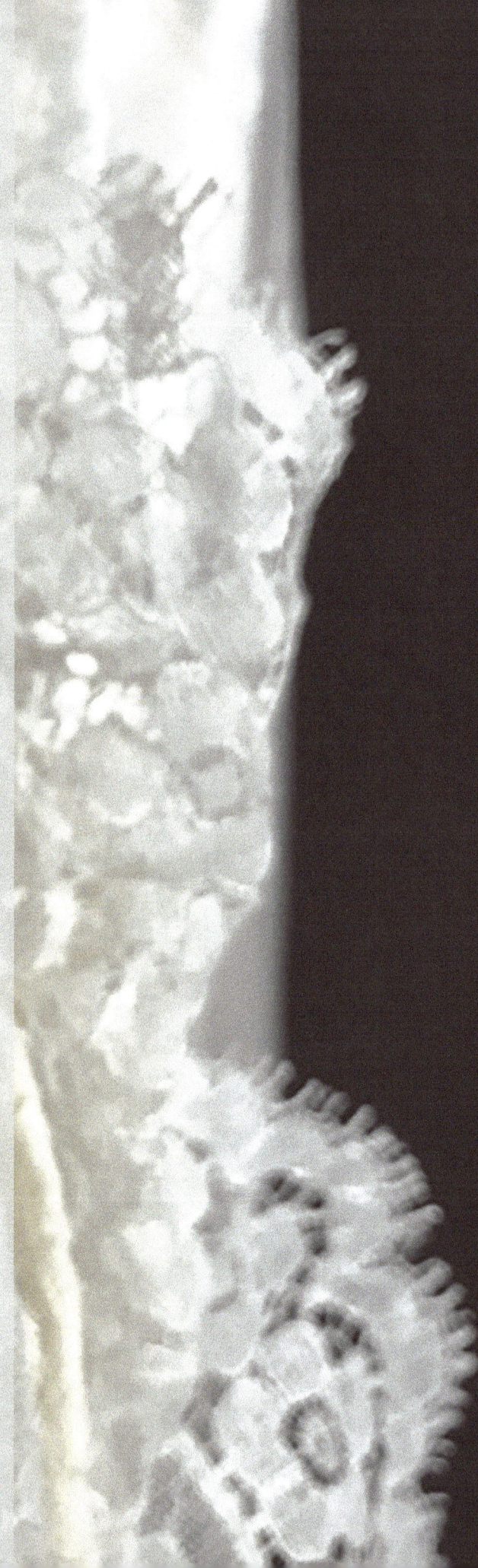

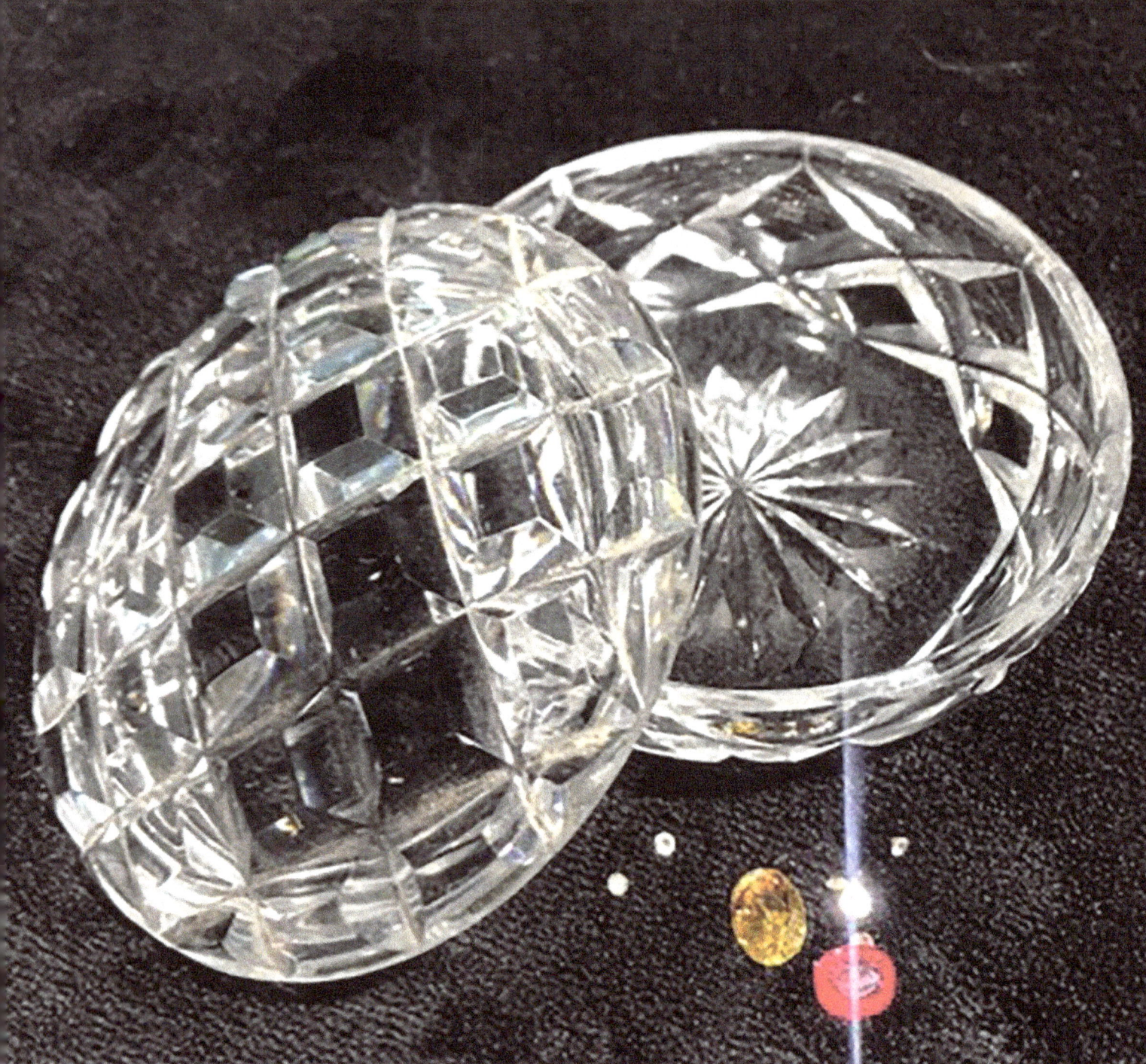

DEBBIE'S WEDDING GIFT

This is a small 5-inch diameter crystal dish with a lid embellished with diamond shapes. The dish contains a few loose crystals, diamonds and rubies that are believed to have originated from the jewelry Elizabeth housed in the crystal jewelry box when in her possession. This item was gifted to Elizabeth from Debbie Reynolds as a wedding present when she married Eddie Fisher.

Source: Roni Howard, Elizabeth Taylor's pay clerk (1947-1972).

This is a personally signed image of Elizabeth on the set of *Cat on a Hot Tin Roof*.

Also pictured is an original porcelain tribute to Elizabeth's role in *Cat on a Hot Tin Roof* (1958).

Source: Screen Stars magazine/MGM.

"Suddenly Last Summer" marked Elizabeth's second collaboration with Montgomery Clift and her first alongside Katherine Hepburn. Despite the film's controversial themes—cannibalism, homosexuality, and insanity—Elizabeth was initially cautioned against taking the role. Yet, against the odds, it turned out to be a brilliant decision.

Both Hepburn and Taylor earned Academy Award nominations in 1959.

Elizabeth's electrifying performance in "Suddenly Last Summer" outshone Marilyn Monroe's, propelling her to her third Academy Award nomination and her inaugural Golden Globe win.

Following her Golden Globe triumph, Elizabeth embarked on two film projects in 1960: an uncredited role in Jack Cardiff's "The Scent of Mystery" and the challenging role of Gloria in Daniel Mann's "Butterfield 8", where she portrayed a prostitute, a role she initially hesitated to accept due to her reservations.

In addition to her film ventures, Elizabeth also graced the small screen with a guest appearance on the BBC show What's My Line?"

THE ELEGANT BLACK LYCRA ELBOW-LENGTH GLOVES

These exquisite elbow-length black gloves were cherished possessions of Elizabeth Taylor herself. Crafted from a sleek black-coated fabric, these gloves exude sophistication and grace.

Elizabeth adorned herself with similar gloves on numerous occasions, from signing her monumental "Cleopatra" contract to attending glamorous galas alongside her beloved husband, Mike Todd.

These gloves also made a stunning appearance in her iconic portrayal of Gloria in the 1960s film "Butterfield 8".

Their timeless elegance and association with one of Hollywood's most legendary figures make these gloves a true marvel of fashion history.

Source: Hollywood Props.

Elizabeth Taylor: My Celebrity Connection

130 | *Elizabeth Taylor: My Celebrity Connection*

Another celebrity doll replicates the likeness of Elizabeth in her role as Gloria in *Butterfield 8* (1960).

Source: Tri- Star/MGM.

Elizabeth Taylor: My Celebrity Connection

Elizabeth is pictured here accompanied by gossip columnist Hedda Hopper, as they make their way to Maxim's Restaurant, Paris, on November 27, 1960.

This is a very rare and exclusive, one-off candid shot of Elizabeth, taken through the limousine window by an adoring fan.

GRAY FAUX-POODLE-FUR CAPE

This silver-gray faux-poodle-fur cape/jacket is lined with silver satin. It was originally gifted from Elizabeth to her long-time hairdresser Sydney Guilaroff.

Guilaroff worked with Elizabeth on many films through the 1960s and mid-70s.

Source: Sydney Guilaroff estate (1995).

During the filming of "Butterfield 8", Elizabeth faced a daunting battle with pneumonia, an illness that had struck her just a week before the tragic loss of her husband, Mike Todd.

The world watched anxiously as Elizabeth fought for her life, and her remarkable recovery transformed her into a symbol of resilience and strength.

The public rallied around her, turning "Butterfield 8" into a monumental success and earning Elizabeth her fourth Academy Award nomination.

On April 18, 1961, still in the process of recovering from pneumonia, Elizabeth, accompanied by her devoted husband Eddie Fisher, graciously accepted her first Academy Award for Best Actress.

Her performance in "Butterfield 8" had captivated audiences worldwide, solidifying her reputation as a talented actor beyond her status as a movie star.

With her newfound recognition came a significant shift in Hollywood's perception of Elizabeth. No longer merely a glamorous celebrity, she was now seen as a formidable talent worthy of substantial compensation.

Her bold request for a staggering $1 million salary to star in "Cleopatra" seemed audacious, yet it was met with acceptance by Twentieth Century Fox studios.

Despite her recent health struggles, Elizabeth dove headfirst into the production of "Cleopatra" and was introduced to her co-star, the charismatic Welsh actor Richard Burton.

Their on-screen chemistry was undeniable, and off-screen, their passionate romance captured the world's attention. Critics and paparazzi alike swarmed around the couple, turning "Cleopatra" into the first tabloid film sensation.

The epic production of "Cleopatra" was not without its challenges. Originally slated for a sixteen-week shoot, the film stretched over three years and incurred astronomical costs, making it one of the most expensive movies ever made.

However, Elizabeth's groundbreaking salary deal, which included a percentage of the box office takings, made her, at the time, the highest-paid woman in film history.

When "Cleopatra" premiered in New York on June 12, 1963, it was an unparalleled success, with ticket sales soaring for months. Elizabeth Taylor had not only conquered the silver screen as the legendary Egyptian queen but had also shattered records and redefined the role of women in Hollywood, if not the world.

SEVERE BOUT OF PNEUMONIA

Here is a circular-style brooch with small copper-like leaves, highlighted with many small purple, blue, and mauve Austrian crystals. The brooch was owned by Elizabeth in the 1960s. The brooch then became part of the collection of Carini D. Auhesu, a collector of movie-star memorabilia.

Elizabeth is pictured wearing a brooch very similar, if not the same, as she leaves a London hospital in 1961 after a severe bout of pneumonia.

Source: Rosyn Herman and Co of New York.

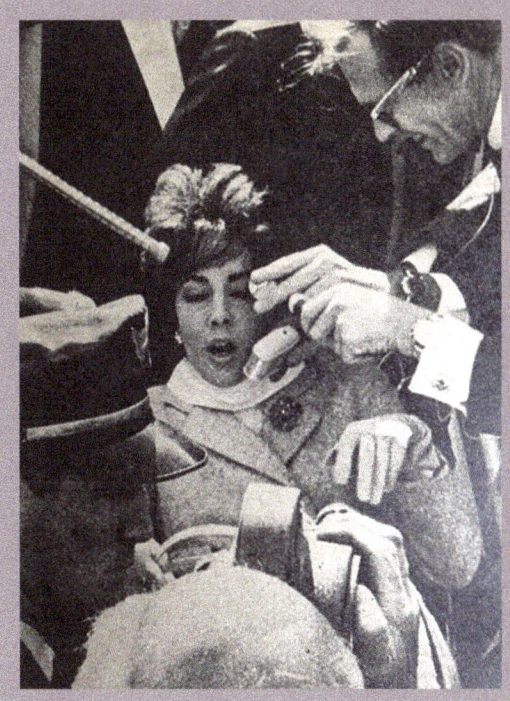

Elizabeth Taylor: My Celebrity Connection

modern screen

DELL

JULY 25¢

LIZ AT HOME

*be with her now
in her most thoughtful moments*

Still bearing the bandages from her tracheostomy operation, Elizabeth chats with several guests at the Coconut Grove Hotel, including Hollywood actor Laurence Harvey (1961).

*I don't really know how to
express my gratitude for this
and for everything.
I guess all I can say is thank you,
thank you from the bottom of my heart.
—Elizabeth Taylor
accepting her Oscar for Butterfield 8.*

THE ASTONISHING EARRINGS OF ELIZABETH TAYLOR

These magnificent teardrop-shaped earrings are a dazzling spectacle to behold, adorned with countless Austrian rhinestones that sparkle with unrivalled brilliance.

While they bear no official markings, experts speculate that they originate from Europe, likely crafted during the late 1950s or early 1960s.

However, their acquisition is believed to have occurred between 1960 and 1970, adding to their mystique and allure.

Legend has it that these extraordinary earrings were acquired by none other than Richard Burton, the legendary actor and Elizabeth Taylor's beloved husband.

Purchased to complement her exquisite ruby necklace, these earrings became a source of amusement for the couple as unsuspecting admirers marvelled at their supposed authenticity.

During a charitable auction attended by luminaries of the silver screen, these remarkable earrings stole the spotlight. Elizabeth, ever the epitome of grace and elegance, graced the stage wearing the earrings, captivating the audience with her radiant presence.

Then, in a moment of unparalleled generosity, she removed the earrings and presented them to the highest bidder, leaving an indelible impression on all who bore witness to her boundless compassion and benevolence.

Source: Personal psychic at the time, Michael J Kouri.

140 | *Elizabeth Taylor: My Celebrity Connection*

During the grand production of "Cleopatra", Elizabeth faced a harrowing trial that threatened to derail the entire endeavour. Just seven months into filming, she succumbed to a severe bout of Asian flu, forcing an abrupt halt to the production as doctors sounded the alarm about her deteriorating health.

As the illness progressed into a perilous case of pneumonia, the gravity of the situation became starkly apparent.

Elizabeth's life hung in the balance, and the prospect of her demise cast a dark shadow over the ambitious cinematic project. With her character's pivotal role in the film, the production faced a daunting dilemma.

On March 28, 1962, after two hundred days of painstaking effort, Twentieth Century Fox and producer Walter Wanger found themselves grappling with an unthinkable reality: not a single frame of usable footage to show for the colossal investment poured into "Cleopatra". The decision was made to relocate the production to Rome, a desperate bid to salvage the monumental undertaking.

Reeling from the dire prognosis delivered by her physicians, Elizabeth embarked on a perilous journey to Rome, where the film sets were painstakingly reconstructed to accommodate her precarious health condition.

Against all odds, the cameras began to roll once more, capturing the indomitable spirit of a star whose unwavering determination defied the spectre of mortality looming over her.

THE ENIGMATIC ELEGANCE OF CLEOPATRA'S GOWN

Amidst the grandeur of "Cleopatra", the costumes emerged as a spectacle in their own right, each embodying a lavish opulence befitting the queen of the Nile. Among the treasures of the wardrobe, one gown stood out—a testament to the meticulous artistry woven into every thread.

Designed by the visionary talents of Irene Sharaff and Vittoria Novaree, this gown epitomised the epitome of elegance, destined to adorn "Cleopatra" in a moment of poignant drama. Adorned in full-length mustard-yellow cotton, it bore the mark of serpentine embroidery, a subtle nod to the queen's mythic allure.

While the costume budget soared to staggering heights and the count reached an impressive 65 ensembles, this particular gown, resplendent in its serpent-like embellishments, held a special allure. Intended for a pivotal scene where Caesar meets his fate in Cleopatra's arms, it exuded an air of regal grace and timeless beauty.

However, fate would intervene, and despite the gown participating in several wardrobe rehearsals it never made it to the final cut.

A piece of Hollywood history destined for the scrapheap.

*Some of the Cleopatra costumes were fun—
they even had real gold threads—
and I wore them as evening dresses afterward!
—Elizabeth Taylor.*

A REGAL RELIC FROM THE SETS OF CLEOPATRA

In the illustrious realm of cinematic history, even the most mundane objects carry a whisper of intrigue, and this rocking chair, steeped in the aura of Hollywood royalty, is no exception.

Nestled within a trailer tailored for the legendary Elizabeth Taylor during the epochal filming of "Cleopatra" in 1963, it bore witness to moments of quiet reflection and intense preparation.

Crafted from the finest Victorian walnut and upholstered in sumptuous celery-green velvet, this diminutive yet opulent nursing chair held a place of honour within Elizabeth's inner sanctum.

In the hushed confines of her trailer, Elizabeth pored over scripts and delved into the depths of her character, perhaps sharing intimate conversations with her esteemed co-star, Richard Burton.

The trailer itself, a marvel of extravagance, spared no expense in catering to Elizabeth's needs, boasting a rumoured cost of seventy-five thousand dollars—an astronomical sum by the standards of its time. As the embodiment of luxury and refinement, it served as a sanctuary for Elizabeth, allowing her to immerse herself fully in the world of the Egyptian queen.

Following the conclusion of filming each night, Elizabeth's trusted double, Michelle Breeze, would find solace in this very chair, continuing the legacy of its occupant. Bearing witness to the ebbs and flows of Hollywood's golden age, it stands as a silent testament to the glamour and magnificence of an era immortalised in this celebrity connection.

Source: United Press International, Heritage Auctions, and the Michelle Breeze estate.

Pictured is the original chair in Elizabeth's movie trailer.

Elizabeth Taylor: My Celebrity Connection

Deduction: MPR - 1%

TWENTIETH CENTURY-FOX FILM CORPORATION
REVISED Synopsis of Employment Agreement

NAME: TAYLOR, ELIZABETH   File No. 5371
                        Contract Closed June 23, 1962
CONTRACT DATE: August 11, 1960; amended July 11, 1961
                        (For closing notice see HUME CRONYN's folder.)

NATURE OF   ACTRESS, to portray leading female role of "Cleopatra"
EMPLOYMENT: in motion picture "CLEOPATRA".

PLACE OF   Miss Taylor's services are to be rendered outside of
SERVICES: United States. Picture will be produced in Italy,
                        with locations in Egypt.

NEW START DATE   September 18, 1961. Miss Taylor agrees to report in
OF SERVICES: Rome on this date.

BASIC COMPENSATION   Miss Taylor acknowledges receipt in full of
HAS HERETOFORE   basic picture price of $125,000.00.
BEEN PAID:

8 FREE WEEKS   Miss Taylor renders services without compensation
SERVICES   during 8-week period commencing September 18, 1961
COMMENCING   and ending November 12, 1961.
SEPTEMBER 18, 1961:

CARRY-OVER RATE $50,000.00 per week and pro rata thereof on basis
AFTER 8 WEEKS   that 1 day equals 1/6 of 1 week.
FREE SERVICES:

RETAKES, ETC. $8,333.33 per day.

TRANSPORTATION and EXPENSES:

20th furnishes first-class round trip transportation from Los Angeles to
Rome (or other place designated by 20th) for Miss Taylor and members of
her family and will reimburse her for traveling expenses incurred by her.

20th furnishes Miss Taylor with a Rolls Royce and full-time chauffeur.

20th pays Miss Taylor $3,000.00 per week for living expenses, including
food and lodging, commencing on date she reports to commence services
and continuing until completion. NOTE: To recoup loan made to Miss
Taylor by 20th of lira equivalent of $27,400.00, the expense allowance
referred to is reduced by $1,500.00 per week in the 18-week period com-
mencing August 28, 1961 (and ending December 31, 1961), and is reduced
by $400.00 in the week following the end of the 18-week period (this
week ends January 7, 1962). Thereafter Miss Taylor's expense allowance
is $3,000.00 per week. (The foregoing was agreed to in letter of August
28, 1961 from Miss Taylor).

TRANSPORTATION, EXPENSES FOR MISS TAYLOR'S AGENT:

If Miss Taylor desires to consult with Kurt Frings while she is on location and agent deems trip necessary, 20th pays Frings' first-class
round trip transportation from Los Angeles to such location, and incident-
al expenses incurred in connection therewith.

9/14/61

This is an extract for Elizabeth Taylor, "Cleopatra' contract dated August 14, 1961. Elizabeth is paid $50,000 per week and $300.00 per week for living expenses, including food and lodging. Any retakes during filming Elizabeth was also paid an additional $8,333.33 per day.

MARVELS FROM THE SANDS OF EGYPT

These four exquisite props, crafted in the style of ancient Egypt, serve as tangible reminders of the opulence and splendour that defined the film's majestic production.

Among these treasures is an Egyptian-style tankard, a vessel fit for a pharaoh's feast, adorned with intricate designs that transport one back to the golden age of the Nile. Accompanying it is a diminutive yet elegant date basket, a symbol of abundance and fertility, meticulously crafted to capture the essence of ancient Egyptian craftsmanship.

But the pièce de resistance is undoubtedly the faux lead knife, wielded with grace and prowess by none other than Elizabeth Taylor herself during filming.

Inscribed with the initials "E. T." atop its blade, this blade exudes an air of authenticity, its handle wrapped in supple leather, its blade tempered to mimic the wear of countless battles and triumphs.

Each of these remarkable artifacts, meticulously crafted by Ellis Props, embodies the attention to detail and commitment to authenticity that permeated the entirety of Cleopatra's production.

From luxuriant tankards to jewelled collars, every prop played a vital role in bringing the world of ancient Egypt to vivid life on the silver screen, contributing to the film's soaring budget in pursuit of cinematic perfection.

Source: Ellis Props/ James McMahan.

Elizabeth Taylor: My Celebrity Connection | 149

This is an original passport application for one of Elizabeth Taylor's sons, Michael Howard Wilding, signed Elizabeth Taylor Fisher and dated August 16, 1961. This allows Michael to accompany Elizabeth on a six month stay in countries listed.

Elizabeth's and Richard's authentic autographs on the set of *Cleopatra* (1963).

I had first met Richard when I was 19. He flirted like mad with me, and I thought, "I'm not going to be another notch in your belt." Little did I know.
—Elizabeth Taylor

He had a wife at the time, she had a husband, they were madly in love.

—Sydney Guilaroff, 1964

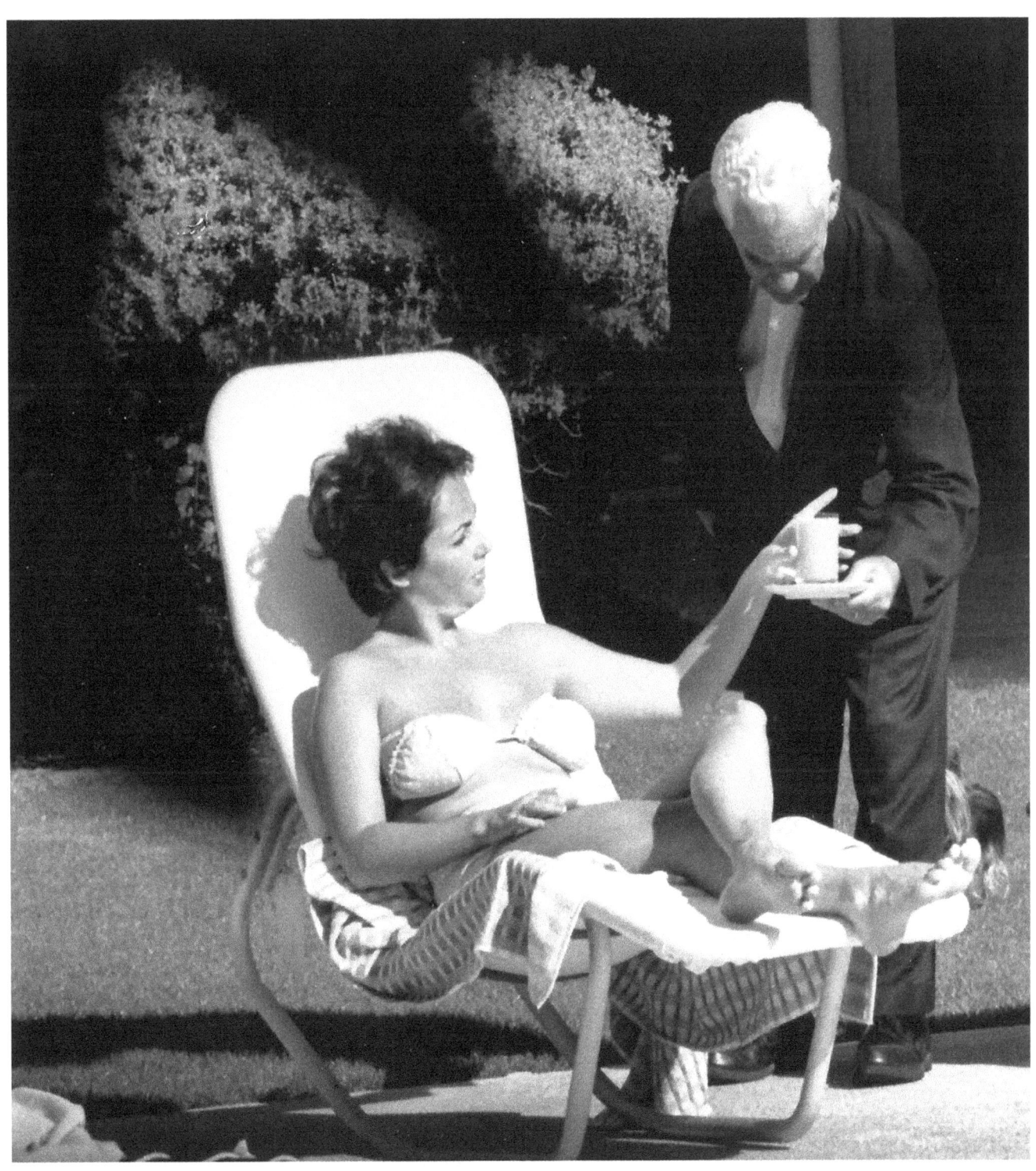

The Lost Paparazzi Shots

At 10:30 a.m. on December 9, 1963, Elizabeth relaxes in the backyard of 1315 Manzanta Avenue, Palm Springs, California.

Source: Gene Daniels/Black Star.

Elizabeth Taylor: My Celebrity Connection

ELIZABETH, POOLSIDE, 1963

Elizabeth and Eddie Fisher are pictured here relaxing in the backyard of their rented house in Palm Springs, and Elizabeth is served poolside by her butler.

The 1960s was the beginning of paparazzi photography. It would follow Elizabeth for the rest of her living days and claim her as one of the most-photographed women in history.

Source: Gene Daniels/Black Star.

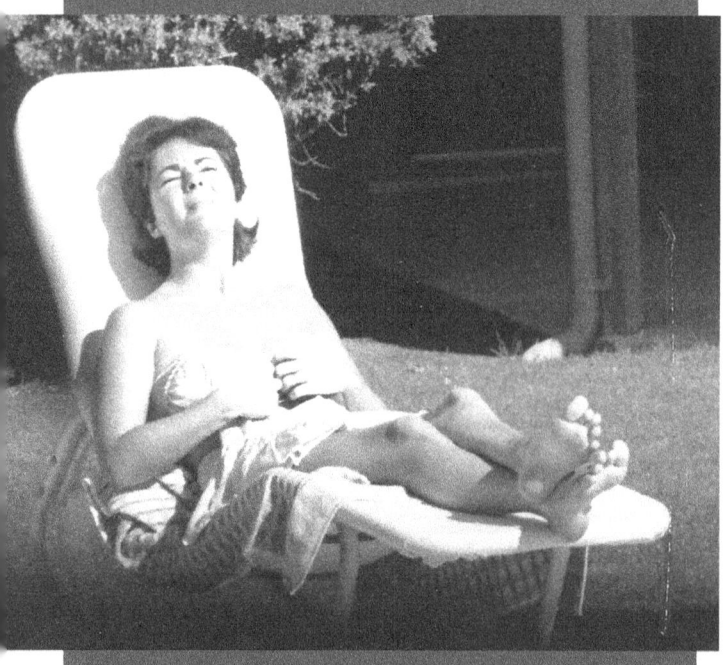

MAKEUP ARTIST TO THE STARS

This is a dark-blue crepe hat with pink flower accent. The hat was gifted from Elizabeth to makeup artist to the stars, Ben Nye. It was then sourced from Star Past Inc. film historians and memorabilia experts.

Hollywood makeup artist Ben Nye enhanced Elizabeth's beauty in *Cleopatra*.

Source: From Ben Nye personal collection/ Star Past Inc. film historians and memorabilia experts since 1987.

CREAM WOOLEN TROUSERS

Pictured here is a pair of cream woolen pants that were owned and worn by Elizabeth and formed part of her wardrobe in the 1960s. Elizabeth is pictured here wearing similar, if not the same, trousers. They have been worn by Elizabeth and show wear on the inside lining.

Source: Julien's Auctions, California.

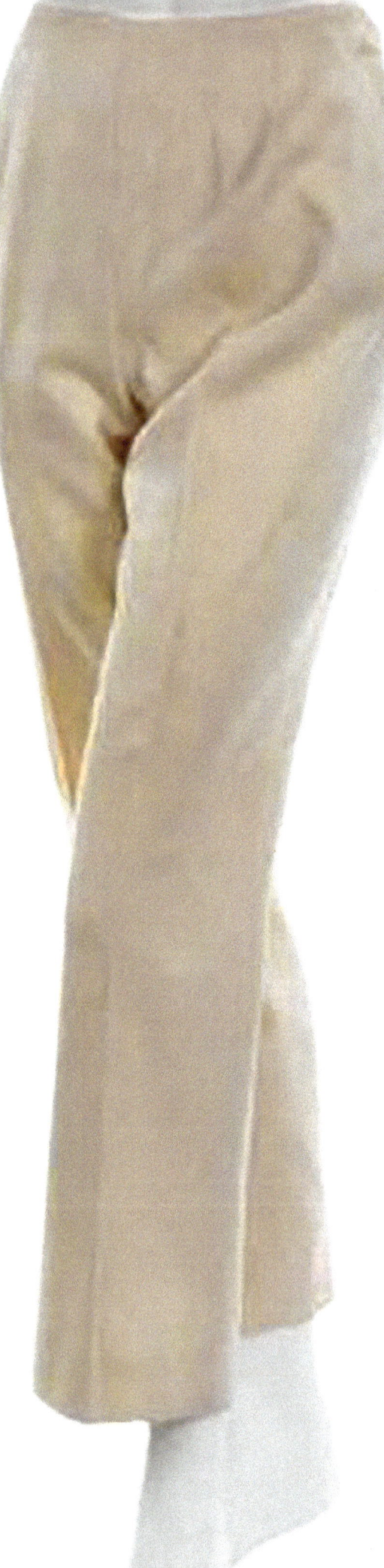

ENCHANTMENT IN BLOOM: THE LILY OF THE VALLEY WEDDING

Picture the scene: March 6, 1964, in Mexico. Elizabeth Taylor, resplendent in a daffodil chiffon dress adorned with delicate lily of the valley flowers in her hair, stood poised to embark on a new chapter of her storied life. As she exchanged vows for the fifth time, a sense of disbelief mingled with elation, captured in her embrace with her new husband, Richard Burton.

"Darling," Mrs. Richard Burton whispered, her voice filled with wonder, "I cannot believe it is really true that we are now husband and wife." The air crackled with the electricity of newfound love, sealing their bond amidst the fragrant blooms of lily of the valley.

With the ink barely dry on their marriage certificate, Richard Burton returned to the set of "Hamlet in Toronto", while Elizabeth immersed herself in the glamorous world of MGM's "The V.I.P.s", bedecked in luxurious furs and jewels that symbolised the union of Taylor-Burton.

Their love, a turbulent storm, often played out on screen and off. Eleven movies bore witness to their fiery passion, mirroring the tumultuous yet magnetic bond between Elizabeth and Richard. Legend has it that "Mr. and Mrs. Taylor" would secure entire hotel floors to shield their passionate arguments from prying ears, a testament to the intensity of their love.

In 1964, the Burtons crafted a sanctuary in the idyllic village of Court Henry, Wales, a $200,000 haven fortified with high walls, a shimmering swimming pool, and state-of-the-art security systems. Here, amidst the tranquil Welsh countryside, the Taylor-Burton saga unfolded in all its captivating complexity, a love story for the ages.

I'm so happy you won't believe it, this marriage will last forever.
— Elizabeth Taylor

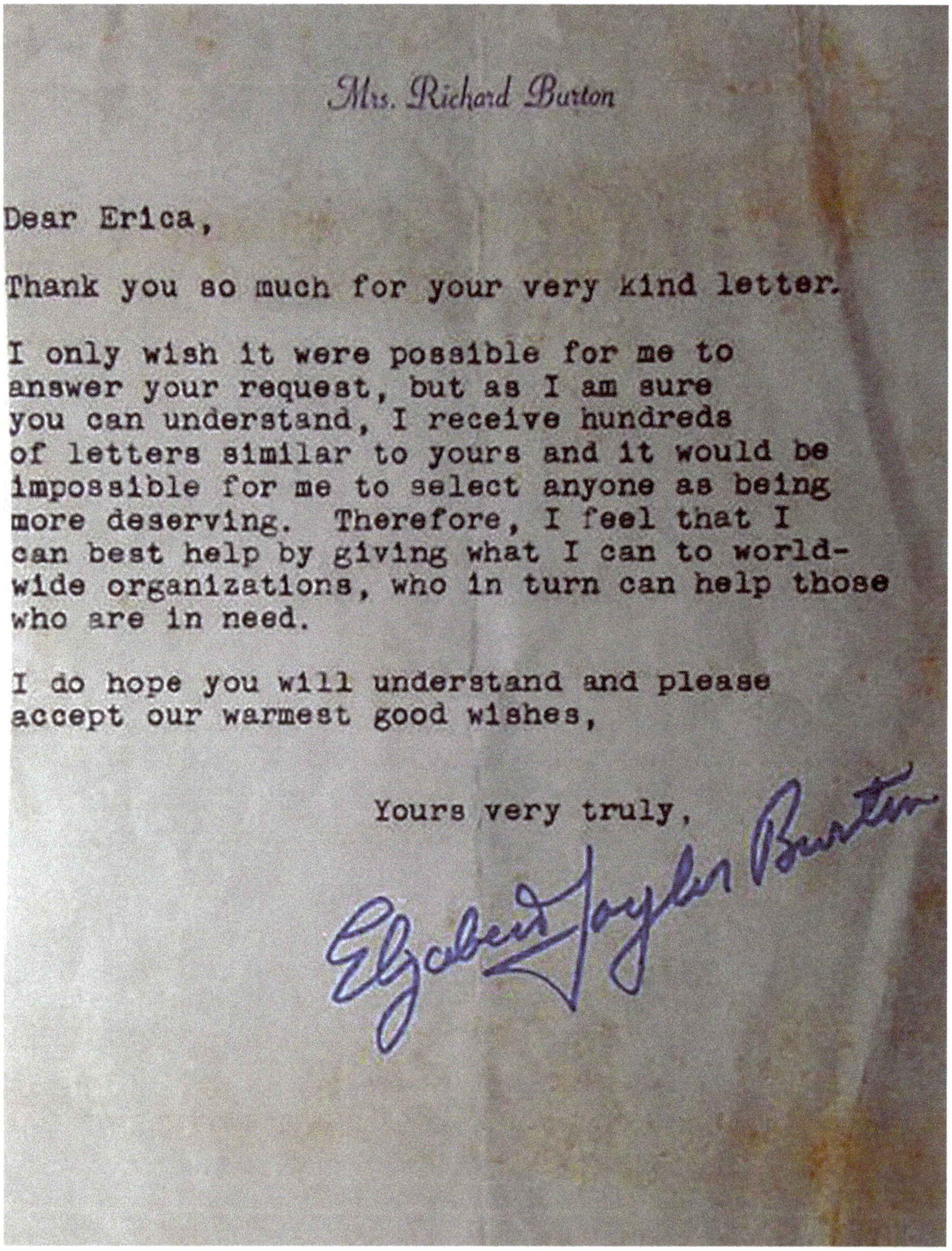

Mrs. Richard Burton

Dear Erica,

Thank you so much for your very kind letter.

I only wish it were possible for me to answer your request, but as I am sure you can understand, I receive hundreds of letters similar to yours and it would be impossible for me to select anyone as being more deserving. Therefore, I feel that I can best help by giving what I can to world-wide organizations, who in turn can help those who are in need.

I do hope you will understand and please accept our warmest good wishes,

Yours very truly,

Elizabeth Taylor Burton

AN UNFORGETTABLE GESTURE: NATIONAL VELVET GIFTED BY MRS. RICHARD BURTON

In 1972, Elizabeth graced a fundraiser event known as the North American Riding for the Handicapped with her presence, radiating her trademark charm and grace. Among the attendees was Jane McClary, who found herself touched by a gesture of unparalleled generosity from the Hollywood icon.

As the fundraiser unfolded, the timeless classic "National Velvet" illuminated the screen, casting its enchanting spell on the audience.

Little did Jane know that this cinematic gem would soon become a cherished keepsake, gifted to her by none other than Elizabeth herself.

But the journey of "National Velvet" to Jane's hands was a tale in itself. Prior to its presentation at the fundraiser, the film had embarked on a remarkable voyage, sent to none other than Mrs. Richard Burton aboard the Taylor-Burton yacht, Kalizma—a vessel named in honour of their beloved daughters.

Encased within this original container are the very reels that traversed oceans to reach Elizabeth's hands, personally addressed to Mrs. Richard Burton.

These reels, designed for 8-millimeter projectors, carry with them the cinematic magic of "National Velvet", captured in each frame.

In a candid moment Elizabeth sits with Jane immortalising yet another heartwarming connection forged through the magic of cinema and the boundless generosity of Mrs. Richard Burton.

Elizabeth Taylor: My Celebrity Connection

Even during a press conference held at the Beverly Hills Wilshire Hotel, Elizabeth reflects a private feeling for her new husband Richard Burton, 1964.

Later that year, Elizabeth and Richard are held up by the media, as they try to board a train in Cardiff for the rugby.

Source: Gene Daniels/Black Star.

162 | *Elizabeth Taylor: My Celebrity Connection*

*I'm so happy you won't believe it—
this marriage will last forever.
—Elizabeth Taylor*

I miss you like something awful—
for some reason especially today—
so be all loving and tenderness tonight please
and if you play your cards right
I will take you out to dinner.
—A love note from Elizabeth to Richard.

MRS. BURTON'S PRIVATE JET

Mr. and Mrs. Burton make their way from the aircraft to the terminal where Richard is sorting out an issue with his passport (1964).

Source: Gene Daniels/Black Star.

Elizabeth Taylor: My Celebrity Connection

Elizabeth and pooch, Theresa, get ready to reboard their aircraft (1964).

166 | *Elizabeth Taylor: The Celebrity Connection*

The correct way to enter your aircraft
with your loving pooch, Elizabeth Taylor Burton (1964).

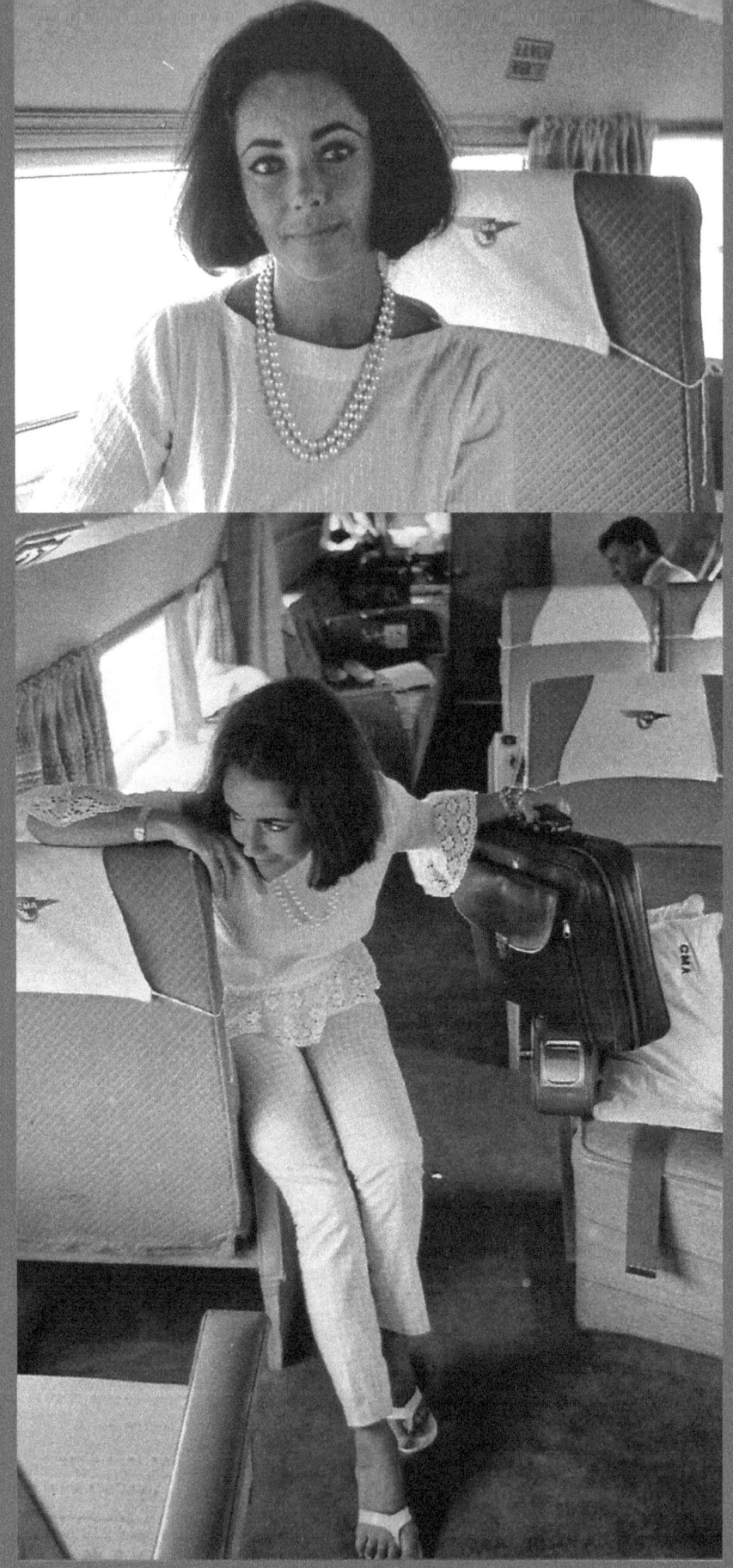

A secret look at the inside of the
Taylor–Burton's private jet (1964).

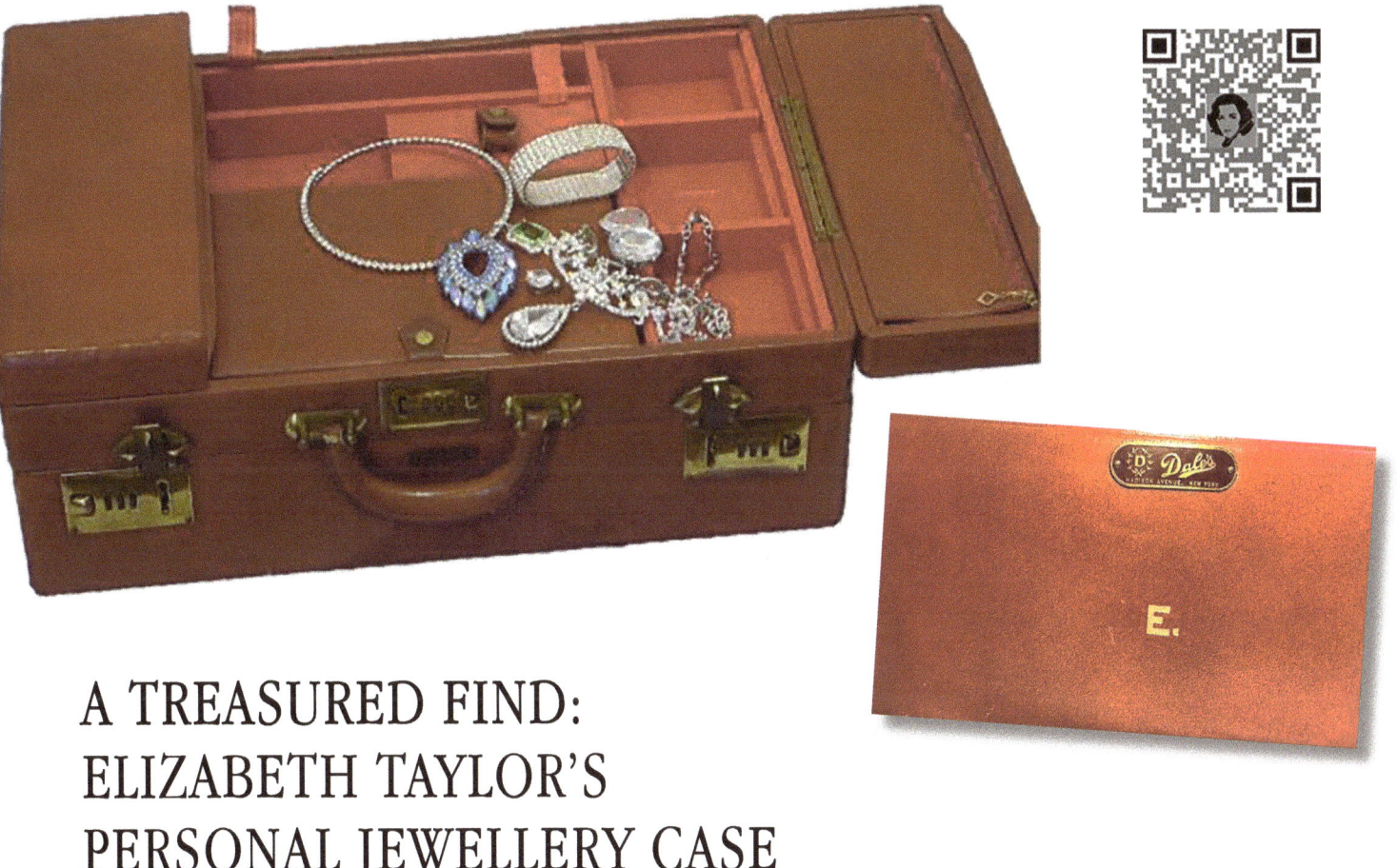

A TREASURED FIND: ELIZABETH TAYLOR'S PERSONAL JEWELLERY CASE

Step into the world of luxury and elegance with this exquisite brown leather jewellery case, a timeless piece that once belonged to none other than the legendary Elizabeth Taylor. Crafted around 1965, this case bears the distinguished monogram "E," signifying its esteemed owner.

Measuring a generous 14 inches by 10 inches, this meticulously designed case boasts multiple compartments and zipper pockets, providing a secure haven for precious jewels and trinkets.

Within its luxurious confines, Elizabeth entrusted her most cherished pieces, each one a testament to her unparalleled style and sophistication.

The journey of this remarkable artifact is as fascinating as its illustrious owner. Collector Barry Weiss, known for his keen eye and passion for unique finds, had the privilege of being invited to Elizabeth's estate after her passing.

Barry recalls the kindness of Elizabeth's associates during the acquisition, although bound by a confidentiality agreement that veiled the finer details of the transaction in secrecy.

Renowned as the "eccentric collector" on the reality television series Storage Wars, Barry Weiss's encounter with Elizabeth Taylor's jewellery case adds yet another chapter to the captivating story of celebrity connection.

Source: Dales, Madison Avenue, New York/ Elizabeth Taylor's estate and Barry Weiss.

Elizabeth Taylor: My Celebrity Connection

In the wake of her second book's publication, aptly titled Elizabeth, and the joyful addition of her fourth child, Marie Burton, Elizabeth found herself immersed in a pandemonium of activity.

Elizabeth's indomitable spirit and insatiable passion for her craft led her to yet another cinematic masterpiece: the 1965 film "The Sandpiper". Directed by the illustrious Vincente Minnelli, this marked Elizabeth's third collaboration with the renowned filmmaker, promising another dazzling performance.

As the cameras rolled and the spotlight beckoned, Elizabeth's talent shone brighter than ever before. Her portrayal in "The Sandpiper" captured hearts and minds alike, earning her a staggering pay check of $1 million—a testament to her unrivalled stature in Hollywood.

But Elizabeth's artistic pursuits were not confined to the silver screen alone. In a bold move, she ventured into the realm of television, captivating audiences with her presence in the BBC show Elizabeth in London.

For her contributions, she received a handsome sum of $250,000, further solidifying her status as an icon of unparalleled comparison and again leaving an indelible mark on the world of celebrity.

With each new endeavour, Elizabeth continued to defy expectations, leaving an indelible mark on the world of entertainment.

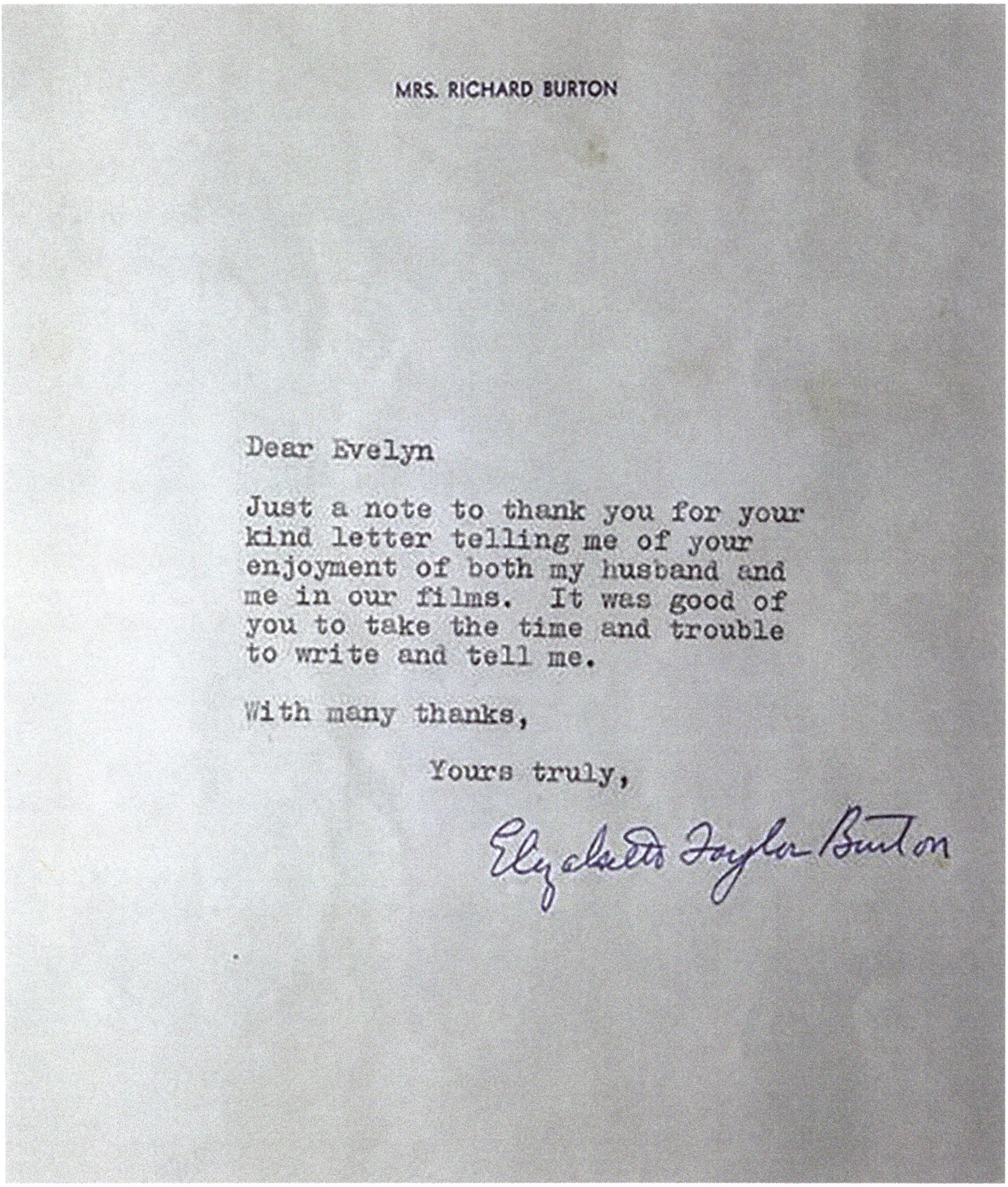

MRS. RICHARD BURTON

Dear Evelyn

Just a note to thank you for your kind letter telling me of your enjoyment of both my husband and me in our films. It was good of you to take the time and trouble to write and tell me.

With many thanks,

Yours truly,

Elizabeth Taylor Burton

Elizabeth replies to a fan (Evelyn), July 16, 1965.

THE POWDER-BLUE COAT

This is a rare powder blue coat with three-quarter sleeves taken straight out of the closet from her Beverly Hills home. The label tells us that it is a "Ben Zuckerman of New York" fashion design, available only at the exclusive Beverly Hills luxury department store, I. Magnin and Company. (This chain started in 1887, was eventually bought by Saks 5th Avenue, and changed its name to Saks around 1994.)

Elizabeth is pictured here in the coat, or if not, similar coat.

It was one of two outstanding coats sold at one of Julien's Auctions of Hollywood Celebrity Memorabilia in 2013.

It was then purchased by Michael and Fredericka Lam, the founders of the Great American Doll Company. In 2017, Michael Lam sold this item to the collector in 2017.

After basking in the glory of her Golden Laurel Award for her captivating portrayal of Laura Reynolds in "The Sandpiper", Elizabeth embarked on yet another remarkable cinematic adventure alongside her beloved husband.

Together, they delved into the depths of their artistry, with Elizabeth bravely embracing the transformative role of Martha in the Warner Bros. masterpiece "Who's Afraid of Virginia Woolf?".

As the cameras rolled and the story unfolded, the lines between reality and fiction blurred, with Richard and Elizabeth immersing themselves so deeply into their characters that it was often difficult to discern where performance ended and reality began. Their commitment to their craft knew no bounds, resulting in a cinematic masterpiece that captivated audiences worldwide.

For her riveting performance, Elizabeth earned not only critical acclaim but also a handsome pay check of $1 million, coupled with a remarkable 10% of the film's gross—a testament to her talent and star power.

A part from that, Elizabeth remained deeply committed to philanthropy, lending her support to worthy causes such as the Thailand Clinic for Emotionally Disturbed Children. Alongside her husband, she helped raise over $100,000 at the prestigious tenth annual Thailand Ball held at the Beverly Hills Hotel—a testament to her compassionate spirit and generous heart.

Soon becoming co-producers, Elizabeth and Richard embarked on a new chapter in their cinematic journey, bringing to life the timeless classic "The Taming of the Shrew" under their Taylor-Burton production banner.

Their collaboration not only showcased their creative prowess but also redefined the boundaries of cinematic excellence, earning them 50% of the net profits from the Columbia Picture release.

TOP SHELF COURVOISIER AND HENNESSEY

Step back in time to the enchanting world of Hollywood's golden era with this exquisite 1960s vintage drinking glass, adorned with an enchanting Egyptian theme.

Crafted with meticulous attention to detail, it features intricate Egyptian figures, symbols, and cartouches set against a mesmerising white-on-olive-green background—an artistic masterpiece that transports you to a bygone era of glamour and sophistication.

Standing tall at approximately seven inches, this glass exudes an air of timeless elegance, with its vibrant colours and impeccable condition adding to its allure.

While devoid of any maker's mark, its craftsmanship bears a striking resemblance to the renowned glassware produced by Hazel Atlas—a testament to its quality and craftsmanship.

But what truly sets this glass apart is its storied history, intertwined with the illustrious career of Hollywood icon Elizabeth Taylor. During breaks on the set of the iconic film "Who's Afraid of Virginia Woolf?", Elizabeth would indulge in the finest top-shelf Courvoisier and Hennessey, sipping from this very glass as she immersed herself in the role of Martha.

As the cameras rolled and the scenes unfolded, Elizabeth's connection to this glass became palpable, infusing each sip with a touch of cinematic magic. Whether used off-set between takes or cherished as a memento of her time on set, this glass bore witness to the legendary actress's extraordinary talent and enduring legacy.

Following the completion of filming at the iconic Red Basket Tavern in Southern Massachusetts, Elizabeth parted ways with this cherished glass—whether intentionally as a heartfelt gesture to owner Lillian Glick or inadvertently, the mystery remains unsolved.

One memorable incident lingers in Lillian's memory—the scene where Martha speeds away from the tavern, only to be pursued by Lillian's spirited dog, prompting multiple reshoots and a chorus of laughter on set.

Source: Lillian Gluck, owner and manager of the Red Basket Tavern, Southern Massachusetts in 1965.

A TREASURED RELIC: TIFFANY & CO. MONEY CLIP

This magnificent treasure is from the illustrious halls of Tiffany & Co.—an original sterling-silver money clip bestowed upon the esteemed cameraman Alfred Daniel Baalas in the wake of cinematic triumph.

Crafted with exquisite precision and bearing the timeless mark of Tiffany & Co., this precious artifact serves as a testament to the enduring legacy of Hollywood's golden era.

Emblazoned with Alfred's initials "A. B." on its back, this sterling-silver masterpiece holds within its gleaming embrace a wealth of memories and gratitude.

Alfred, a stalwart of the Technicolor Picture Corporation, lent his expertise to the filming of the iconic "Who's Afraid of Virginia Woolf?" alongside the legendary Elizabeth Taylor.

Alfred's journey in the world of cinema traces back to his tenure alongside Elizabeth's third husband, the visionary Mike Todd, during the production of "Around the World in 80 Days".

A testament to his dedication and talent, Alfred's contributions to the realm of filmmaking earned him the esteemed honour of being entrusted with this cherished keepsake.

In a gesture of heartfelt appreciation, Elizabeth herself hosted an unforgettable soirée at her opulent Hollywood estate following the completion of "Who's Afraid of Virginia Woolf?", extending a warm invitation to the dedicated crew who brought the film to life.

Elizabeth presented Alfred with this gleaming token of gratitude, a symbol of her profound admiration and appreciation for his invaluable contributions to the cinematic masterpiece.

Though Alfred may have departed this world on February 28, 2006, his legacy lives on through this exquisite Tiffany & Co. money clip—a tangible reminder of his unwavering dedication to the craft of filmmaking and his enduring bond with one of Hollywood's most iconic figures.

Source: Alfred Daniel Baalas estate/ Victoria L Johnson, niece to Alfred Daniel Baalas.

Elizabeth Taylor: My Celebrity Connection

THE SYMBOL OF EVERLASTING LOVE: THE KRUPP DIAMOND

In the whispers of romantic gestures, few can rival the breathtaking tale of Richard Burton's acquisition of the legendary Krupp diamond—an exquisite testament to the enduring bond between him and his beloved Elizabeth. This platinum-mounted marvel, resplendent with an emerald-cut diamond, stands as a shimmering symbol of their profound and unyielding love.

Venturing into the hallowed halls of the Parke-Bernet Galleries on Madison Avenue, Richard Burton embarked on a journey of unparalleled devotion as he placed a bid at the Highly Important Jewels auction on May 16, 1968.

With each tender stroke of his bidding paddle, he sought to encapsulate the depth of his affection and admiration for his cherished wife in the radiant brilliance of this remarkable gem.

While the Krupp diamond served as a tangible manifestation of Richard's adoration for Elizabeth, its significance transcended mere material wealth. For myself, its acquisition held a deeply personal connection—a celestial alignment of destiny that intertwined with their own life story.

Knowing that this iconic jewel had been secured on my birthday infused the moment with an aura of celestial serendipity, and celebrity connection.

With a price tag of $385,000, the Krupp diamond stood as a testament to the unparalleled beauty and rarity of true love.

Renowned as one of the most flawless diamonds in the world, its resplendent allure captivated all who beheld its radiant splendour.

According to Elizabeth herself, this dazzling gem was her prize for triumphing over Richard in a spirited game of ping-pong—a whimsical testament to the playful camaraderie that enriched their enduring union.

SALE NUMBER 2703

FREE PUBLIC EXHIBITION

From Saturday · May 11 to Date of Sale
10 a.m. to 4:45 p.m. ∤ Closed Sunday and Monday

OPEN TO DEALERS ONLY ∤ MONDAY · MAY 13 FROM 10-3 P.M.
ADMISSION ON PRESENTATION OF BUSINESS CARD

PUBLIC AUCTION

Thursday · May 16 at 10:30 a.m. and 1:45 p.m.

EXHIBITION AND SALE AT THE
PARKE-BERNET GALLERIES · INC

980 MADISON AVENUE · 76TH-77TH STREET

NEW YORK 10021

TELEPHONE: 212/879-8300

∤ ∤ ∤

Sales Conducted by
PETER WILSON · JOHN L. MARION
CHARLES A. HELLMICH · EDWARD LEE CAVE
EDWARD J. LANDRIGAN III

1968

In the extraordinary lifestyle that was Elizabeth Taylor, few jewels shine as brightly as the fabled Elizabeth Taylor Diamond—a magnificent 33.19-carat (6.638 grams) gem that once bore the weighty legacy of the Krupp Diamond.

Steeped in history and imbued with profound symbolism, this illustrious stone embarked on a transformative journey that mirrored the indomitable spirit of its iconic owner.

For Elizabeth, the acquisition of the Krupp Diamond was more than a mere act of indulgence—it was a triumph over history itself. Recalling the diamond's sinister past as a wartime relic, Elizabeth mused, "How perfect it would be if a nice Jewish girl like me were to own it." And so, in a thrilling bidding war that pitted her against the formidable Harry Winston, Elizabeth emerged victorious, claiming the diamond as her own and forever banishing its shadowy past.

From that moment forth, the Elizabeth Taylor Diamond became more than just a precious gem—it became a cherished symbol of resilience, defiance, and triumph over adversity. Rarely leaving Elizabeth's finger, it bore witness to the highs and lows of her extraordinary life—a steadfast companion in an ever-changing world.

In the late 1960s, as Elizabeth and Richard Burton navigated the tumultuous waters of Hollywood, their on-screen collaborations mirrored the complexities of their off-screen romance. From forgettable roles in "Doctor Faustus" to the halting reception of "The Comedians:, the couple faced their fair share of challenges.

As the years passed, Elizabeth weathered personal tragedies with grace and resilience. The loss of her father, Francis, in 1968 and the untimely death of her first husband, Conrad Nicky Hilton, in 1968 marked profound moments of sorrow. Yet, Elizabeth's indomitable spirit remained unbroken, her flame burning ever brighter in the face of adversity.

In 1971, as Elizabeth dazzled audiences with her unparalleled talent in "Zee and Co", co-star Michael Caine found himself captivated by her brilliance. Despite sharing the screen with a myriad of leading ladies throughout his career, Caine declared Elizabeth the most impressive of them all—a testament to her enduring legacy as one of Hollywood's true luminaries.

Travelling into the future the gavel would fall at Christie's auction house on December 16, 2011, the Elizabeth Taylor Diamond claimed its place in the annals of history, fetching a staggering $8,818,500—a testament to its enduring allure and the timeless legacy of its illustrious namesake.

The story of this remarkable gem stretches far beyond the confines of a glittering auction house, intertwining with the narrative of Elizabeth's own remarkable journey.

I remember I was doing a film with Elizabeth a long time ago and didn't know what to expect—lots of tantrums, probably. But she was completely professional, knew her lines before she turned up, never had a temper tantrum, she was quite amazing.
—Sir Michael Caine

HOSTING HOLLYWOOD PARTIES

This is a '60s/'70s vintage David Brown-I. Magnin California-label lounge-wear hostess dress. A white-and-red-dotted maxi dress. Dots are in varying sizes, which were inspired by Op-Art.

Elizabeth was extremely well known and liked both for her great acting accomplishments and for her charity activities, which she pursued into her final days. This and other comfortable and loose-fitting elegant hostess gowns were often worn by her as she hosted many Hollywood parties and innumerable charity events. Julien's describes the gown as "a graphic white floral print on a navy background, zip front, and matching belt." It has "David Brown" and "Magnin" labels, marked "Size M." Most of Elizabeth's David Brown hostess designs were purchased at this world-famous luxury Beverly Hills store, I. Magnin.

It just personifies her life and her style, even in her later years, and just creates its own subtle yet elegant ambience around it. We can only fantasize how she may have looked and felt wearing this as she casually mingled with her friends over cocktails and hors d'oeuvres at a midafternoon Beverly Hills pool party.

Source: Julien's Celebrity Auction in Beverly Hills/ Michael and Fredericka Lam, the founders of the Great American Doll Company.

SAKS FIFTH AVENUE

Here are a pair of Elizabeth's owned beautiful bright-red wool trousers. This is a pair of bright-red trousers labelled "Saks Fifth Avenue the Young Circle." No size present.

Source: Julien's Auctions in California /Jill's Treasures.
Jill sold them onto the collection in 2017.

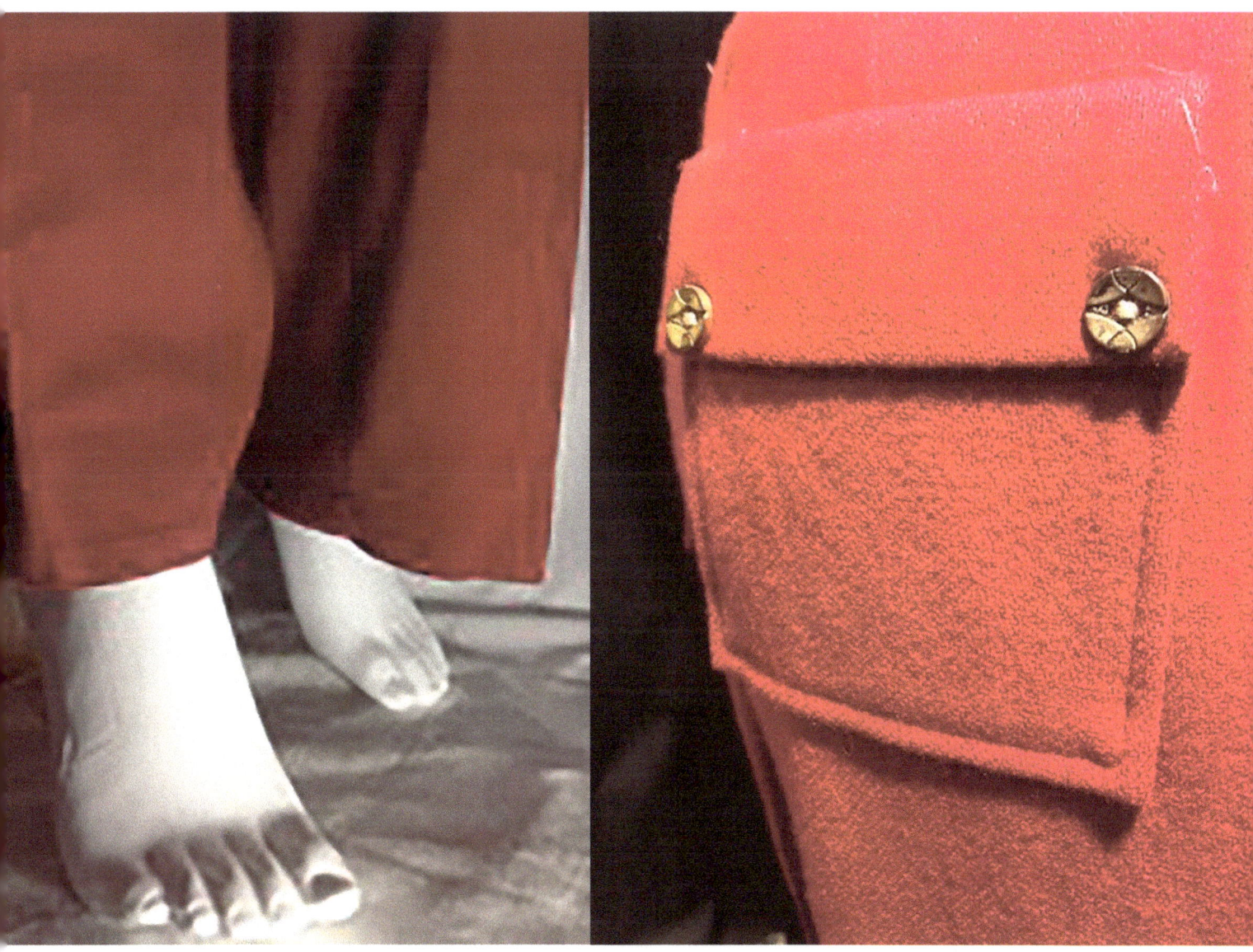

LEOPARD SKINS

This is a replica of the original leopard-fur jacket gifted to Elizabeth by Richard Burton in June of 1963. It has been reported that the coat was specially made for Elizabeth from the skins of five South American leopards.

Source: Morocco, styled by Sportowne. Fabric by La France/Wire Photo's (1968).

ELIZABETH IN MIND

This Nolan Miller faux-sapphire-and-diamond flower brooch is adorned with gold petals, embellished with crystal rhinestones, and is highlighted with a faux sapphire in the centre. Length is 2.5 inches and height is 1.75. Nolan designed this brooch with Elizabeth in mind.

Source: Nolan Miller estate.

THE ICONIC DIRECTOR'S CHAIR OF E. T. B

In the intricate web of Hollywood history, few artifacts resonate with the same aura of majesty as the director's chair of E. T. B.—an emblem of Elizabeth Taylor's legendary presence on the silver screen.

Steeped in the glamour of Tinseltown's golden age, this chair bore witness to the filming of "Hammersmith Is Out", where Elizabeth's luminous talent illuminated the screen alongside her then-husband, Richard Burton.

Crafted with the elegance befitting a Hollywood icon, the chair stands taller than the average, its wooden frame painted a sleek black, with a luxurious grey vinyl seat and backrest offering comfort amidst the whirlwind of film production.

It is the small black plastic placard adorning the left arm—bearing the initials "E. T. B."—that elevates this humble seat to the realm of cinematic legend, marking it as the throne of Hollywood royalty.

During the filming of "Hammersmith Is Out:, Elizabeth's performance as Jimmie Jean Jackson captivated audiences and critics alike, earning her the prestigious Silver Berlin Bear award for Best Actress at the esteemed Berlin International Film Festival.

As she breathed life into her character, the chair stood as a silent witness to her brilliance—a testament to her unparalleled talent and enduring legacy.

Following the completion of production, Elizabeth, ever generous in spirit, bestowed the chair upon her stand-in and dear friend, Michelle Breeze, ensuring that a piece of Hollywood history found a worthy home.

Decades later, the chair emerged from the shadows of memory, consigned to Heritage Auctions in 2017.

Source: Heritage Auctions, Texas/ Michelle Breeze estate.

Elizabeth is pictured here using the actual director's chair whilst taking a break on set of *Hammersmith Is Out*, with director, Peter Ustinov.

A SPLASH OF MULTI-COLOURED GLAMOUR

In Elizabeth Taylor's wardrobe, each garment tells a story of glamour, style, and the allure of Hollywood's golden era. Amongst her treasures, this vibrant multi-coloured floral bathing suit stands out as a testament to her timeless elegance and enduring charm.

Crafted from a luxurious cotton-blend fabric, this one-piece bathing suit was Elizabeth's trusted companion during sun-drenched holidays with her beloved husband, Richard Burton. Its fishbone bodice and sewn-in undergarment offered both style and comfort, ensuring Elizabeth radiated effortless beauty whether lounging by the pool or frolicking on sandy shores.

As with many of Elizabeth's personal garments, this bathing suit bears no maker's name or size—a nod to the mystique and allure of Hollywood's elite. In an era where secrecy shrouded celebrity fashion, Elizabeth's sartorial choices remained a tantalising enigma, inspiring admiration and emulation from fans around the world.

Joseph King, renowned makeup artist to the stars, shared a special bond with Elizabeth, collaborating on countless film projects throughout her illustrious career. Recognising Joseph's passion for collecting mementos from his celebrity clients, Elizabeth bestowed upon him this exquisite bathing suit as a cherished souvenir of their time together—a token of their enduring friendship and shared love for the magic of Hollywood.

Elizabeth Taylor: My Celebrity Connection | 187

VICTORIO & LUCCHINO

This is a ten-tier cotton-lined cream laced skirt that flows to the floor. The skirt was purchased by Elizabeth during a holiday visit to Spain in the 1970s. It became a part of her personal wardrobe and was later gifted to J. Madeleine Munoz, who was part of the Taylor staff for over seventeen years.

Victorio & Lucchino is an Andalusian fashion firm, which takes its name from those of its creators, José Víctor Rodríguez Caro Victorio and José Luis Medina del Corral Lucchino.

They began their journey in the world of fashion in the late 1970s in the city of Seville. At the beginning of the seventies, Victorio joined Lucchino to present his own collections under the name of Victorio & Lucchino.

Source: Marina Del Rey California

Elizabeth Taylor: My Celebrity Connection | 189

STROLLING THE STREETS IN PLAID

These plaid woolen pants labelled "Saks Fifth Avenue," size 10, came from the personal wardrobe of Elizabeth, originally sourced by Julien's Auctions, California, from the home of Elizabeth Taylor. Elizabeth is pictured strolling the streets with her then-husband Richard Burton and wearing similar-, if not the same, style trouser.

Source: Jill's Treasures/ Jill's Treasures sells celebrity-owned item.

190 | *Elizabeth Taylor: My Celebrity Connection*

While Elizabeth Taylor and Richard Burton's cinematic endeavours may have faltered, their opulent lifestyle captured the imagination of the world, casting them as Hollywood's most glamorous couple. Before Hollywood had "Brangelina", it had "Liz &Dick".

Nestled within the sun-kissed landscapes of Puerto Vallarta, Mexico, their sprawling estate, the Case Kimberly Estate, stood as a testament to their unparalleled luxury.

Two magnificent houses, connected by a bridge, formed the backdrop of their extravagant lifestyle. Elizabeth's abode, on the left, mirrored her husband's on the right—a symphony of elegance and grandeur.

Within the confines of Elizabeth's private sanctuary, her bathroom exuded an aura of indulgence, adorned with her Favorite fragrance, Gardenia. Each scent-laden breath whispered tales of beauty and allure, enveloping her in a cloud of timeless sophistication.

Their final cinematic collaboration, "Divorce His, Divorce Hers," unveiled the complexities of their real-life drama on the silver screen. Portraying a couple torn asunder by indifference, quarrels, and infidelity, the turbulent echoes of their own marriage. As the credits rolled, the curtain fell on their eighteen-year union, culminating in Elizabeth's decisive step to part ways with her fifth husband on June 26, 1974.

Undeterred by the shadows cast by their personal lives, Elizabeth embarked on a cinematic odyssey, starring in four films between 1973 and 1974. Yet, despite her efforts, critics dismissed her performances as mere pedestrian strolls through the park.

I won't be a puppet anymore.
—Elizabeth comments on her divorce
from Richard Burton.

A LOVE STORY ETCHED IN PINK

In the confines of Elizabeth Taylor and Richard Burton's romance, Casa Kimberly emerged as a beacon of their extravagant love. Nestled amidst the cobblestone streets of Puerto Vallarta, Mexico, this $40,000 villa stood as a testament to their enduring passion.

It was Richard Burton's gift to Elizabeth, a token of his affection during their sojourn to Puerto Vallarta while he filmed "The Night of the Iguana." With its quaint charm, the sleepy fishing village transformed into a bustling tourist destination, thanks in part to the allure of Burton and Taylor's romantic escapades.

Casa Kimberly, adorned with seven bathrooms and seven bedrooms, served as their sanctuary. Yet, even this lavish estate proved insufficient for the fervour of their love. Across the street, another villa beckoned—a mirror image of their affections, connected by a delicate pink bridge reminiscent of Venice's Bridge of Sighs.

Legend has it that when the couple sighed in each other's presence, Burton would find solace in the doghouse across the bridge.

Their love, tumultuous yet undeniably passionate, echoed through the halls of Casa Kimberly from 1968 to 1975, a testament to their fiery romance.

Elizabeth, the custodian of their love nest, held onto the four-story abode until 1990. When she bid farewell, she sold it in its entirety, furnishings and all, leaving behind traces of their love—clothes in the closets, and personal photographs adorning the walls.

Today, Casa Kimberly stands as a living testament to their immortal love story. Transformed into a restaurant and accommodation complex, it pays homage to the iconic lovers whose passion once graced its halls.

Within the echoes of their laughter and whispers of affection, Casa Kimberly remains a cherished chapter in the legacy of Elizabeth Taylor and Richard Burton—an ode to love, immortalized in shades of pink.

THE ASHTRAY

This hand-engraved sterling-silver ashtray once belonged to Elizabeth. Both Richard Burton and Elizabeth were heavy smokers during their time together, so much so that it is believed that Richard went and had an ashtray especially made for Elizabeth with her name engraved.

The ashtray is engraved "Elizabeth" in the style of Taylor's signature and believed to have been a birthday gift from Richard. The ashtray is stamped to verso with "Allan Adler Sterling." Interestingly, the design is based on a small tray in Adler's regular range, with two cigarette holders added on opposite corners.

Allan Adler was an American silversmith, known as Silversmith to the Stars. Beginning his career as an apprentice in 1938, Adler designed silverware in shapes inspired by the Modernist art movement of the early 1900s. Other items he made included a silver belt for singer Michael Jackson and a silver lunchbox for Carol Channing, who carries the tin to banquets and awards shows.

Source: Julien's Auctions, USA/ Casa Kimberly Estate, Puerto Vallarta, Mexico.

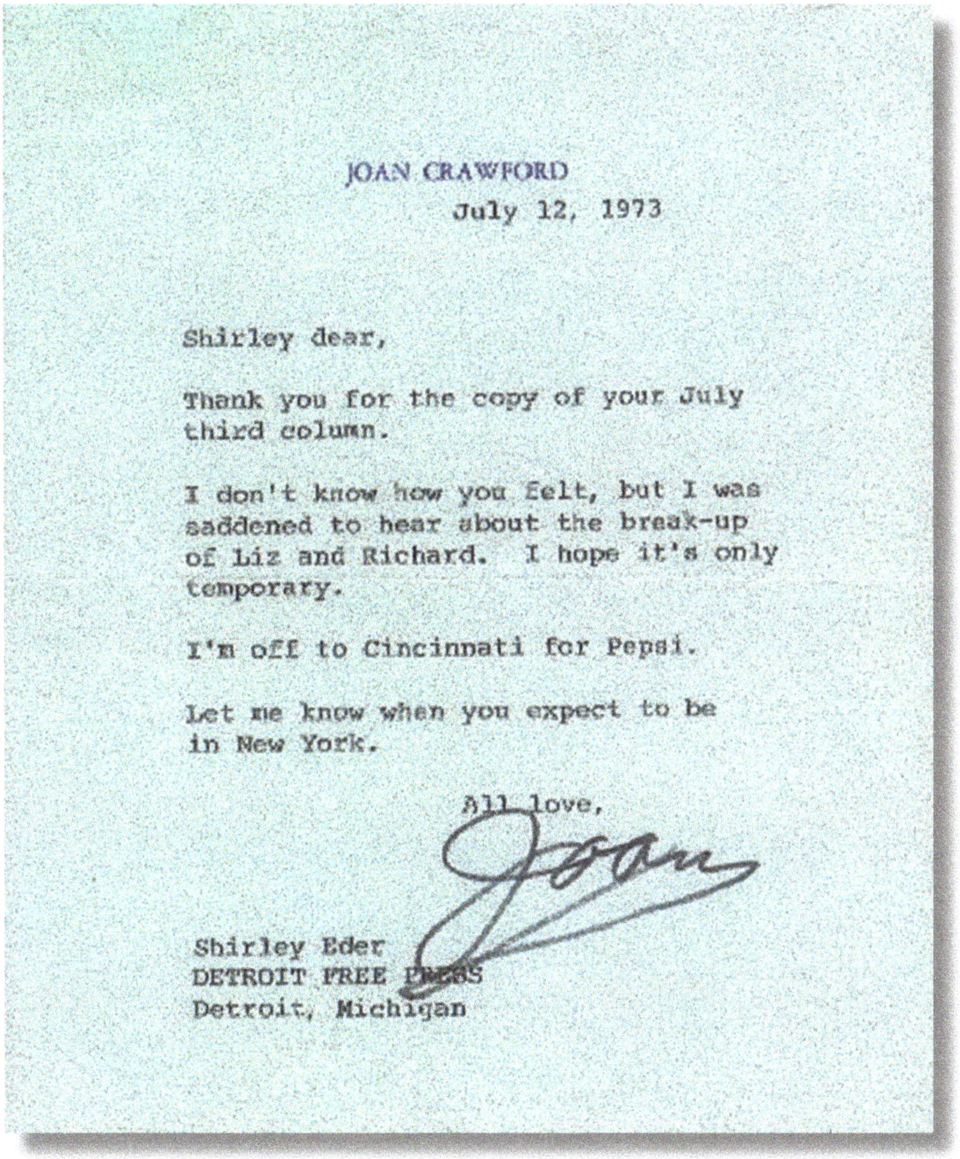

> **JOAN CRAWFORD**
> July 12, 1973
>
> Shirley dear,
>
> Thank you for the copy of your July third column.
>
> I don't know how you felt, but I was saddened to hear about the break-up of Liz and Richard. I hope it's only temporary.
>
> I'm off to Cincinnati for Pepsi.
>
> Let me know when you expect to be in New York.
>
> All love,
> Joan
>
> Shirley Eder
> DETROIT FREE PRESS
> Detroit, Michigan

In a letter from Joan Crawford dated July 12, 1973, Joan speaks of her feeling on the separation of Elizabeth and Richard.

COLLECTION OF HEAD SCARVES

These head scarfs were once part of Elizabeth's personal Casa Kimberly wardrobe.

The first scarf is a psychedelic-yellow floral-patterned design on a white background. Each end of the scarf is embellished with white tassels. It is made by Italian and Paris designers H. Bubois & Co.

The second is a multicoloured dotted design, including white, yellow, pink and orange dots on a pink background, which has no label.

Source: The personal wardrobe of Elizabeth Taylor during her residency with Richard Burton at Casa Kimberly Estate, Puerto Vallarta, Mexico (1977)/ Christiana Auction Gallery, Newark.

196 | *Elizabeth Taylor: My Celebrity Connection*

PSYCHEDELIC FLOWERS AND SWIRLS

This maxi dress is part of a collection of three worn by Elizabeth during her residence at Casa Kimberly, Mexico. This long-sleeved maxi dress is printed with colourful psychedelic flowers and swirls. The cuffs are heavily embellished with large rhinestone, faux crystals, bugle beads, sequins, and palettes.

Source: The personal wardrobe of Elizabeth Taylor during her residency with Richard Burton at Casa Kimberly Estate, Puerto Vallarta, Mexico (1977).

GEMMA TACCOGNA

This is a set of two vintage Gemma Taccogna paper-mache figurines. One represents a female form and the other a cat. Both figurines are designed to hold pencils. Both are handpainted with bright colours and lacquered. These figurines once adorned the shelves of the Casa Kimberly home of Elizabeth. Imagine the stories they could tell if only they could talk or even write with the pencils they carried.

Source: Gemma Taccogna paper-mache figurines/ Casa Kimberly Estate, Puerto Vallarta, Mexico (1977).

ENTERTAINING GUESTS

This beautiful clear-glass container/ice bucket with silver-plated rim and lid measures 6 inches in circumference and is 7 inches tall. Elizabeth and Richard entertained guests on the veranda of their Casa Kimberly estate.

Source: Julien's Auctions California, Gene Daniels/Black Star.

THE PERSIMMON BACKGROUND

This is a sleeveless dress with a colourful ethnic print on a persimmon background, also from the Casa Kimberly story. No size or label present.

Source: The personal wardrobe of Elizabeth Taylor during her residency with Richard Burton at Casa Kimberly Estate, Puerto Vallarta, Mexico (1977)/ Julien's Auction House, Los Angeles.

Elizabeth Taylor: My Celebrity Connection | 201

BOUQUETS OF VIOLETS

This dress labelled "By Nelly" is from a group of three worn by Elizabeth during her residence in Mexico. This powder-blue cotton shirt dress is embroidered with bouquets of violets. When Elizabeth sold the house, she left all her belongings, pictures, and clothing there. She said it was too painful to be there after Richard Burton died.

Source: The personal wardrobe of Elizabeth Taylor, during her residency with Richard Burton at Casa Kimberly Estate, Puerto Vallarta, Mexico.1977/Julien's Auction House, Los Angeles.

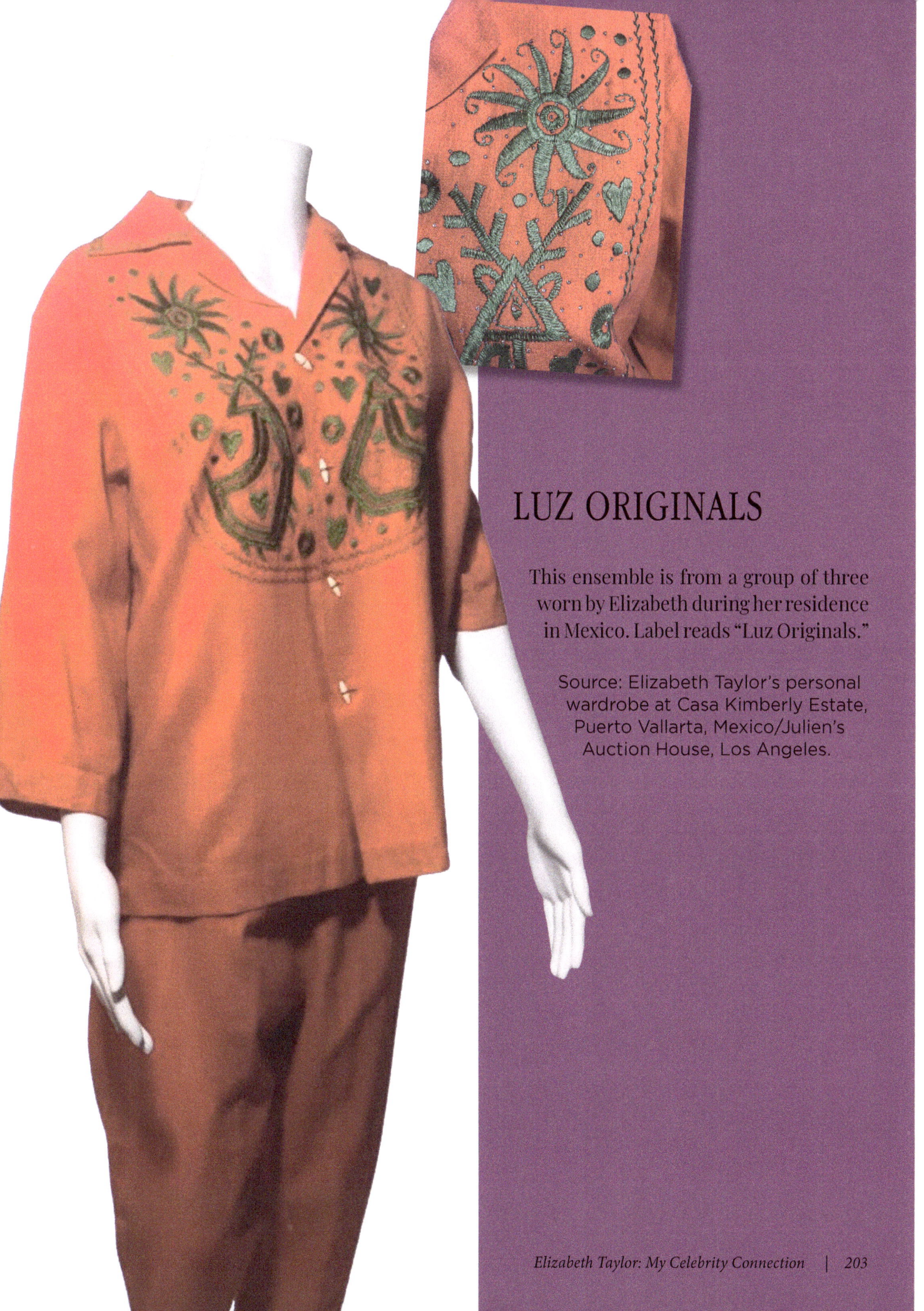

LUZ ORIGINALS

This ensemble is from a group of three worn by Elizabeth during her residence in Mexico. Label reads "Luz Originals."

Source: Elizabeth Taylor's personal wardrobe at Casa Kimberly Estate, Puerto Vallarta, Mexico/Julien's Auction House, Los Angeles.

Elizabeth Taylor: My Celebrity Connection

THE EMBROIDERED BLOUSE

This is a white cotton blouse embroidered with orange and yellow flowers with faux ivory buttons.

Source: The personal wardrobe of Elizabeth Taylor, during her residency with Richard Burton at Casa Kimberly Estate, Puerto Vallarta, Mexico.1977/ Julien's Auction House, Los Angeles.

ELIZABETH'S LAVENDER CRYSTAL PERFUME BOTTLE

Here is a relic of timeless elegance—a lavender crystal perfume bottle that once graced the delicate hands of Elizabeth Taylor herself. This exquisite piece, a symbol of beauty and refinement, found its way into the possession of Gordon Bau, the maestro behind Elizabeth's captivating makeup during the filming of "Who's Afraid of Virginia Woolf?"

Gordon Bau, revered as the luminary of Warner Brothers' makeup department from the 1930s to the '70s, was entrusted with Elizabeth's radiant allure in 1966. As a token of gratitude for his artistry, Elizabeth bestowed upon him this ethereal perfume bottle—a vessel of transcendent allure.

Crafted from crystal of the purest lavender hue, this bottle embodies sophistication in its very essence. Its graceful silhouette, standing five inches tall with a three-point shape, captivates the eye with its subtle allure. Adorned with a crystal lavender stopper, it whispers secrets of fragrant gardens and whispered promises.

Within its delicate confines once dwelled Elizabeth's beloved fragrance—Gardenia—an olfactory symphony of floral enchantment. Little did she know that this cherished possession would later inspire the design of the iconic Passion perfume bottle, perpetuating its legacy for generations to come.

In the timeless dance of beauty and artistry, Elizabeth's lavender crystal perfume bottle remains a testament to her enduring elegance—an artifact of enchantment.

Source: Gordon Bau Estate/ Roslyn Herman Antique and Collectables.

206 | *Elizabeth Taylor: My Celebrity Connection*

THE 1972 PREMIERE

This privately owned and used purse containing two movie-ticket stubs suggests Elizabeth went to a movie using the handbag. Price per movie ticket reads 20 cents.

This Whiting and Davis Alumesh off-white handbag is inspired by the mesh pouch bag first designed by Paul Poiret in 1929.

Today Whiting and Davis still produce metal mesh in Massachusetts and have become renowned for their supply of mesh fabric for film garments and advertising campaigns.

Mr. Sydney Guilaroff was given the item as a memento after doing Elizabeth's hair for a premiere she attended in 1972.

Source: Originated from estate of Sydney and Jose Guilaroff. Later John Le Bold and Film Historian and Memorabilia Expert acquired the item. It was sold to the collection in 2010.

Elizabeth Taylor: My Celebrity Connection

In 1975 while being absent from the silver screen, Elizabeth grabbed the world attention as she embarked on a passionate rollercoaster ride and emotional romance, that would have rivalled the most dramatic of any Hollywood prop.

Briefly entwined in a romance with Henry Weinberg, Elizabeth's heart remained tethered to the one true love of her life—Richard Burton.

Their bond, tumultuous yet undeniable, defied reason and logic, embodying a love story for the ages. In a stunning turn of events, Elizabeth and Richard exchanged vows once again on October 10, 1975, sealing their reunion with a promise of eternal devotion.

Like a tempestuous storm, their love was both fierce and fleeting. In a mere eight months, the echoes of their laughter faded, drowned out by the weight of their differences.

The couple, unable to bridge the chasm between them, parted ways for the second time on July 26, 1976, leaving behind a trail of broken hearts and shattered dreams.

But Elizabeth, ever resilient, found solace in the arms of Senator John Warner—a welcome respite from the tumultuous sea of emotions she had weathered with Richard.

With grace and elegance, she embraced a new chapter in her life, exchanging vows with Senator Warner on December 4, 1976. Dressed in a knee-length cashmere dress, adorned with a tweed coat trimmed in grey fur, and clutching a bouquet of wild heather, Elizabeth radiated timeless beauty and poise.

As whispers of her romance with Senator Warner echoed through the halls of fame, Elizabeth's professional endeavours continued to captivate audiences around the world.

In 1976, she graced the silver screen alongside Edward Lewis and director George Cukor in "The Blue Bird"—a groundbreaking cinematic masterpiece that transcended borders as the first Soviet-American co-production in film history.

SOUTHERN FRIED CHICKEN

This is a scarf made by H. Dubois and Co. It is a black-and-daffodil-yellow plaid scarf with hand-rolled edges with a label that reads "Handwoven in France for H. Dubois and Co, Paris. Elizabeth is pictured here cooking her favorite Southern fried chicken at Atoka Farm, Middleburg, Virginia, 1976, in a similar, if not the same, scarf.

Source: Julien's Auction House, Los Angeles/FirooZ Zahedi.

RITZ HOTEL IN PARIS, 1976

This is a Valentino two-piece tan cotton-blend vest and pant suit, comprising of a button- down vest with envelope pockets and matching trousers. Label reads "Valentino." Elizabeth is pictured wearing the outfit as she attends a costume fitting for the movie *The Blue Bird* at the Ritz Hotel in Paris in 1976. Some years later, Princess Diana would be captured on CCTV leaving the Ritz Hotel in Paris shortly before her death in a car crash in 1997.

From the auction of the collection of Elizabeth held to raise funds for the Elizabeth Taylor AIDS Foundation after her passing in 2011.

Source: Christies Auction House, Los Angeles.

Elizabeth Taylor: My Celebrity Connection | 211

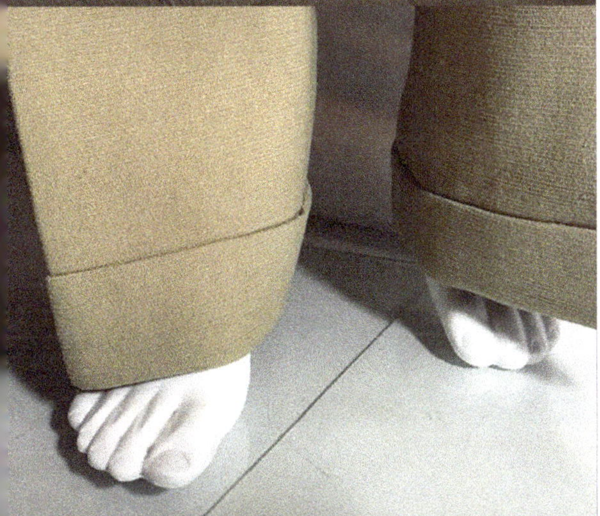

Elizabeth was once again immortalised in the doll form, which resembled more of her home life seen on the farm with John Warner than on the silver screen.

Source: Horsham/Len Film Organisation.

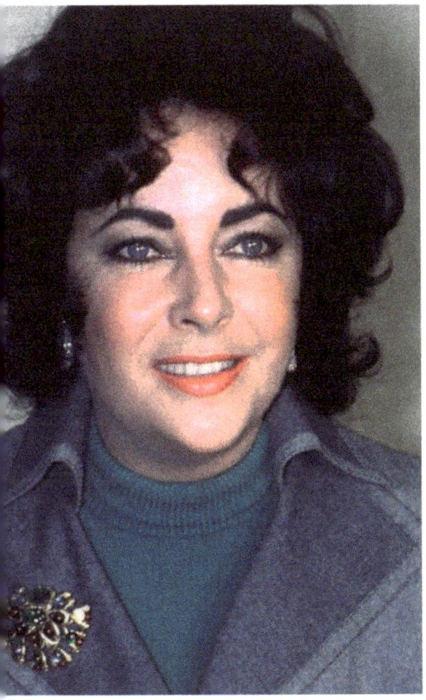

VALENTINO

This dark-green Valentino turtleneck sweater comes from the wardrobe of movie-legend Elizabeth Taylor (1979). Elizabeth is seen here, wearing a turtleneck.

Source: Disneyland Attractions/Peter Boulin.

Elizabeth Taylor: My Celebrity Connection | 213

In 1978, Elizabeth made a captivating return to the silver screen, enchanting audiences with her presence in the dazzling realm of musicals through Harold Prince's production of "A Little Night Music."

Her performance was a breathtaking spectacle, as Elizabeth unveiled her vocal prowess in a mesmerizing rendition of "Send in the Clowns," stirring souls with unparalleled grace and emotion.

As the curtain fell on one chapter of Elizabeth's life, another unfolded with profound generosity and compassion. In 1979, amidst whispers of her legendary jewels, Elizabeth made a monumental decision—to part ways with the iconic Taylor-Burton diamond.

But this was no ordinary sale; it was a gesture of unparalleled altruism. With unwavering determination, Elizabeth announced her intention to use a portion of the proceeds to fund the construction of a children's hospital in Botswana—a beacon of hope for generations to come.

In a crescendo of philanthropy and magnanimity, the Taylor-Burton diamond found a new home in the hands of Henry Lambert, a New York jeweller, who seized the opportunity to acquire the illustrious gem for an astonishing $5 million.

Thirteen stone, that's a boiling piece that came with many unkind jokes.' The one I heard most, "Elizabeth was seen in town today wearing a yellow dress, and school children were running to the bus to board her."
— Elizabeth Taylor

I wanted to grow old with somebody, on the farm, in front of the fire place and read books.
— Elizabeth Taylor

The Taylor-Burton diamond is sold to raise funds to build a children's hospital (1979).

THE CHIFFON EVENING GOWN

This is an authentic, beautiful full-length pink layered chiffon gown. It appears to have been custom made, as it is unlabelled and no size is evident. Elizabeth appears in a gown similar, if not the same, with then-husband John Warner on the cover of *People* magazine on October 20, 1980.

The gown was given to Sydney Guilaroff, who worked with Elizabeth on many of her films, including *The Blue Bird, Who's Afraid of Virginia Woolf?* and *The Sandpiper*, among a few.

Source: Sydney Guilaroff estate (1988).

Elizabeth Taylor: My Celebrity Connection | 217

BUTTERFLIES AND CIRCLES

This is a short-sleeved A-line dress. It ties at the front and is printed with large butterflies and circles on an emerald and white background.

Label reads "Frankie Welch." It was designed by Frankie Welch, who is a designer best known for printed scarves and the gown Betty Ford wore to her husband's presidential inauguration. A sketch by an unknown designer captures Elizabeth Taylor Warner's fashion sense at the time.

Source: Julien's Auction House, Los Angeles.

Elizabeth Taylor: My Celebrity Connection | 219

THE MARABOU HOUSE SHOES

As Mrs. Warner, Elizabeth was often required to invite other senators, politicians, and candidates to the Warner estate in Middleburg, Virginia. On occasion and wearing these gorgeous kitten heels, Elizabeth was known to have casually sashayed down the stairs to her waiting guests, where she would pretend to have lost an earring or other precious jewel and would have men scampering at her feet in search of it, only to find out moments later that Elizabeth had the item in her possession the whole time.

These amazing pink satin and marabou kitten heels or house shoes where originally acquired by Elizabeth from Fredericks of Hollywood.

They were later consigned from the Georgetown Emporium, Virginia.

In 1981, Elizabeth Taylor, adorned with the title of a senator's wife, embarked on a journey onto the Broadway stage, under the dazzling lights of Zev Buffman's production of "The Little Foxes." It was a revelation, a resplendent moment where the allure of the stage breathed new life into Elizabeth's fading career.

As she graced both Broadway and the West End with her presence in the 1982 revival of Lillian Hellman's "The Little Foxes," she simultaneously delved into the preproduction of Noël Coward's "Private Lives," reuniting once more with the enigmatic Richard Burton.

Surrounded by the applause and acclaim of the theatre world, Elizabeth's heart yearned for the serenity of the countryside. With the season's end of "The Little Foxes," she retreated to the quiet embrace of her farm, grappling with the weight of personal tribulations that threatened to engulf her spirit. In the throes of emotional turmoil, she bestowed upon herself the moniker of "Boiling Piece," a poignant reflection of her inner turmoil.

Yet, even as she navigated the tumultuous seas of chronic health issues and the relentless demands of public life, Elizabeth's resilience remained unyielding. With a steadfast resolve to reclaim her essence, she sought solace in the familiar embrace of Frank Sinatra's former abode at 700 Nimes Road, Bel Air, California.

In this sanctuary, where echoes of Hollywood's golden age whispered tales of yore, Elizabeth found sanctuary, anchoring herself in the essence of her past.

As the chapters of her life unfolded with both triumphs and trials, Elizabeth Taylor bid farewell to one-chapter, divorcing John Warner on November 7, 1982. It was a testament to her indomitable spirit and unwavering determination to chart her own course amidst the tempests of fate.

*I knew that I was plunging
and the ultimate result would be death,
so I had to do something dramatic
to pull myself out.
I was drinking so much,
so I thought what would be
the most challenging thing to do?*

*When politics came along, John was married
to the senate, I couldn't cope with that.
—Elizabeth Taylor*

Elizabeth holds a press conference during her West End debut in *The Little Foxes* (1982).

Elizabeth Taylor Warner

Dearest John —

John and I will be unable to attend your wonderful Theatre World Award Party on the 25th of May.

My weight is still fucked up and so is the tape on your goddamed answering machine.

...Maybe next year.

Affectionately

Elizabeth Taylor Warner

THEATRE WORLD AWARD PARTY

This precious artifact—a handwritten note from the iconic Elizabeth Taylor, penned during the pivotal years of 1982 to 1983. It was a time when Elizabeth, adorned with the title of Mrs. Elizabeth Taylor Warner, embarked on a remarkable journey back to the limelight, gracing both Broadway stages and the small screen in a triumphant comeback.

This rare gem of a letter, shrouded in the mystery of its undated origins, bears witness to Elizabeth's candid authenticity. In it, she gracefully declines a party invitation with a flourish of colourful language, candidly remarking on her weight at the time—a subject of relentless scrutiny in the public eye.

With characteristic wit, she laments the woes of an inoperative answering machine, offering a glimpse into the everyday trials of a legendary star.

The signature "Elizabeth Taylor Warner" serves as a reminder of her union with Senator John Warner of Virginia, anchoring this artifact firmly within the tapestry of history.

The letterhead, adorned with the same moniker, provides further context to this captivating piece of personal memorabilia.

Indeed, this handwritten note stands as a testament to Elizabeth's resilience, capturing a fleeting moment in time before her triumphant return to the glamour and grandeur that had defined her illustrious career.

In its candid honesty and unfiltered expression, it offers a rare glimpse into the inner workings of a Hollywood legend on the brink of a magnificent resurgence.

LITTLE FOXES

Imagine holding in your hands a piece of theatrical history—a vintage ruby bracelet worn by none other than the legendary Elizabeth Taylor during her Broadway run of "Little Foxes."

This exquisite piece of jewellery, once adorning the wrist of the iconic star as she graced the stage, now serves as a tangible link to the golden age of Broadway.

But what makes this treasure truly remarkable is its journey into the hands of Matilda Kupp, a fortunate recipient of Elizabeth's generosity. Matilda, who had the privilege of assisting Elizabeth during numerous productions, forged a deep bond with the star over the years. In a gesture of appreciation and friendship, Elizabeth bestowed upon Matilda this stage-worn jewel—a token of her gratitude that speaks volumes about their cherished relationship.

As you hold this precious bracelet, envision Elizabeth herself, radiant and captivating, bringing characters to life under the spotlight of Broadway.

Source: Matilda Kupp estate. Sold to this collection by Dave W. Kupp, executor of the estate.

It's hard to believe that even someone as revered as Elizabeth Taylor faced such profound struggles. As she celebrated her fifty-second birthday, she found herself grappling with unbearable pain and inner turmoil, seeking solace in drugs and alcohol.

Hiding in the darkness, Elizabeth showed immense courage by becoming the first star to seek treatment at the Betty Ford Centre for alcohol and drug dependency on December 5, 1983. It was a groundbreaking step, highlighting her determination to confront her demons head-on.

After her release from the centre on December 20, 1983, Elizabeth's battle was far from over. Despite her fierce spirit, she continued to endure severe back pain, which often confined her to a wheelchair in her later years.

Her journey became a poignant reminder of the fragility of even the most iconic figures.

Despite her public image as Hollywood royalty, Elizabeth's struggles with grief and depression were all too real. In her darkest moments, it was said that only food and drink offered her any semblance of comfort.

Yet, through it all, she remained a symbol of resilience and grace, inspiring millions with her unwavering spirit.

*I am so glad that I asked for help,
I was stuttering, stumbling,
and incoherent.
I had used sleeping pills
for over 25 years
I learned to rely on them.
—Elizabeth Taylor*

A CUSTOM-MADE FUR COLLAR

This is an authentic purple waist-length wool jacket with a fur collar. It is embellished with two detailed buttons. The item has no labels or size and has been custom made. It is a jacket that was worn by Elizabeth to a special occasion in 1983. An item originally gifted from Elizabeth to the hairdresser of the star, Sydney Guilaroff, who worked with Elizabeth on many of her films.

Source: Sydney Guilaroff estate (1995).

Elizabeth Taylor: My Celebrity Connection

Elizabeth and Richard arrive
for the final night of *The Private Lives* (1983).

Source: Walter Miller Jr.

230 | *Elizabeth Taylor: My Celebrity Connection*

*He will never ever leave me.
In a way I don't think that
our relationship will ever end.
Two months before
Richard died, he said to his brother,
"Oh that bloody woman, I still love her,
and I know one day I'm going to end up
marrying her again, even if it's in heaven."
We couldn't stay away from each other.
— Elizabeth Taylor.*

LOS ANGELES AIRPORT

This is a pair of beautiful soft black leather boots with three-inch heels used and worn by Elizabeth to the Los Angeles airport in the late 1980s.

Source: Richard Wilson.

This original photograph of Elizabeth and Burt Reynolds was taken by Roddy McDowall at Rock Hudson's Californian estate in 1983.

Source: Rock Hudson Estate/Martin Flaherty.

Elizabeth and good friend Liza Minnelli are pictured here, backstage at an AIDS fundraiser May 5, 1983.

It was remarkable how Elizabeth's life unfolded with a series of so many triumphs and heartaches. In 1984, she made a memorable return to the small screen with a brief but impactful comeback in the made-for-television movie "Between Friends," directed by Lou Antonio.

Additionally, she made a cameo appearance in Vince McEveety's "Hotel," showcasing her enduring presence in the entertainment world.

On August 5 of the same year, her beloved Richard Burton passed away in Switzerland at the age of fifty-nine.

Elizabeth was shattered by the loss of the man she had loved deeply, a sentiment so strong that she had married him twice.

The blows of grief continued to strike. Several months later, she received devastating news of the passing of her former co-star from "Giant," Rock Hudson, on October 2, 1985, from an AIDS-related illness at the age of sixty.

However, rather than retreating into sorrow, Elizabeth channelled her pain into a powerful force for good.

Her love for the silver screen transformed into a passion for human rights, particularly in the realm of AIDS awareness and support.

Despite facing criticism from some quarters, she fearlessly embraced the cause, using her influence to champion those in need of compassion and care.

THROUGH THE LENS OF SADNESS

This is a purple/blue clear pair of sunglasses designed by Laura Biagiotti.

They were owned and worn by Elizabeth (pictured) most memorably when she tried to visit the gravesite of her fifth husband, Richard Burton, in Celigny, Switzerland, in 1984. Some years later, in 1988, Elizabeth is pictured wearing the same glasses as she leaves a Los Angeles hospital in a wheelchair.

Elizabeth donated the glasses to a Celebrity Wares store to help raise money for a local animal shelter.

Source: Star Wares on Main, Santa Monica, California.

Good friends Bob Hope, Shirley MacLaine, and Elizabeth (1985).

Source: Yani Begakis

Rock Hudson's death activated Elizabeth into some kind of movement.

—*Shirley MacLaine*

Elizabeth Taylor: My Celebrity Connection | 239

Elizabeth took to the stage at the Golden Globe Awards, to receive yet another accolade, the Cecil B. De Mille Award, in 1985.

Source: Bob Scott.

Amidst the triumphs and heartaches, it was utterly astounding how Elizabeth retained her celebrity status, with the public's fascination never wavering. In 1985 alone, she clinched two prestigious awards – the Golden Apple award for female star of the year and the Women in Film Crystal Award.

Her trophy cabinet, adorned with accolades since her very first Golden Globe in 1957, boasted over thirty awards, highlighting not only her silver screen prowess but also her profound impact in the eighties.

Elizabeth's transformation from Hollywood screen goddess to activist was awe-inspiring. Embracing causes close to her heart, particularly AIDS charities and human equality, she wielded her fame to challenge the moral fabric of modern society.

With an unwavering determination, she used her platform to raise awareness and funds, laying the groundwork for her life's mission. Leaving behind the glitz of Hollywood, she emerged as a formidable advocate in the battle against AIDS.

In 1985, her involvement in television projects like "Malice in Wonderland" and the miniseries "North and South," alongside Patrick Swayze, wasn't just about performance; it was a beacon of hope. Her fees from these ventures, totalling over $200,000, served as a testament to her boundless generosity and unwavering commitment to her beloved AIDS charity, a cause cherished by all who admired her.

The transformation of Elizabeth from a silver screen icon to a champion of social justice was nothing short of remarkable.

MADAME CONTI

In the mid-1980s, Elizabeth wore a lot of Hollywood-designer Nolan Miller costumes and clothing. He was also famous for the outrageous costumes in the 1980s TV drama *Dynasty*. In her role as Madame Conti in the TV series *North and South*, Elizabeth wore this black velvet gown.

Source: Nolan Miller/Heritage Auction House, Texas.

*I went to a hospice outside of Rome.
It was all AIDS patients,
and the society ladies of Rome
couldn't walk their dogs near this building
because they thought AIDS was
an airborne illness
and that their dogs might catch it.
The ignorance.
I went inside and said,
"Is there anything we can do for you?"
One man said, "To have someone
put their arms around us."
I still feel the stinking of tears in my eyes,
as I kissed each and every one of them.
—Elizabeth Taylor*

244 | *Elizabeth Taylor: My Celebrity Connection*

OSCARS CEREMONY

This is an item donated by Elizabeth to a celebrity store to raise money for a local animal refuge. This evening gown is an off-white crepe style embellished with clear beads throughout. It ties at the waist with a flowing bow. It was created by British designers Elizabeth Florence Emanuel and her former husband David Emanuel, best known for their 1981 work for the wedding of Diana, Princess of Wales.

The gown was designed for Elizabeth to attend the 1985 Oscars ceremony, where she was accompanied by George Hamilton.

Source: Arlyn Rudolph of Celebrity Seconds, Palm Springs, California, sourced this item from the personal wardrobe of Elizabeth Taylor. The item was then sourced for this collection from the Celebrity Seconds store, which has now closed after Elizabeth Rudolph passed away in 2011.

Elizabeth Taylor: My Celebrity Connection

SUNBURST PLEAT AND FULL-LENGTH RUFFLES

When attending the 1986 Oscars ceremony, Elizabeth emerged looking as stunning as ever in this especially designed Nolan Miller gown. The corsage-formed bodice is highlighted with a shirred bustline gigot style, three-quarter-length sleeves. The waist and cuffs are finished with a point, and the back of the skirt features a sunburst pleat between full-length ruffles, adorned with pink silk stemmed roses.

Source: Christie's Auctions/
Nolan Miller estate.

Elizabeth Taylor: My Celebrity Connection | 247

ELIZABETH TAYLOR

February 15, 1985

Ms. Monica Sharp
Great Journeys LTD.
2 West 45th Street
New York, New York 10036

Dear Ms. Sharp,

I would like to extend my very warm thanks for your very kind letter.

I just wanted you to know that you must never throw in the towel - you have to keep working at it - and most important of all you must really want to do it. Unless there is a health reason for your not losing the weight, then keep on trying. Age has nothing to do with it, as I am about to turn 53 and it is only in the past year that I have maintained and worked at keeping it down. I have always had a weight problem - but dedication and determination made it come true.

If I can do it than so can you. I hope that you succeed and I send you my every good wish.

Sincerely,

Elizabeth Taylor

In a letter to a fan (Monica Sharp), dated February 15, 1985, Elizabeth, who is about to turn 53, inspires Monica by sharing words of encouragement around her personal battle with weight and says, "If I can do it, then so can you".

SPAGHETTI STRAPS THAT FLOW TO THE FLOOR

This long flowing sequined evening gown was designed for Elizabeth by Hollywood designer Nolan Miller to wear to the 1986 Oscars Ceremony. She, however, chose another of his designs instead. This Nolan Miller sequined gown has a blouse draped bodice and spaghetti straps that flow to a floor-length flared skirt forming a train.

The gown is of an abstract netting in lavender, gold, and silver, embroidered with gold thread in a meandering line, embellished with sequins in silver and lavender over a lavender crepe lining. The side zipper closure exposes the Nolan Miller label to the rear.

Source: Heritage Auction House, Dallas, Texas/ Nolan Miller estate.

Elizabeth Taylor: My Celebrity Connection

Placid Domingo and Elizabeth at the Franco Feffirelli premiere of *Turandot*, March 12, 1987. Elizabeth would later appear in Zeffirelli's, *Young Toscanini*.

Source: Harmonie Autographs and Music Inc.

In 1986, Elizabeth unveiled her inaugural perfume, Passion, and the world was left utterly spellbound. It skyrocketed to become the highest-grossing celebrity fragrance in history, showering Elizabeth with an astonishing $70 million in its debut year alone.

Even now, decades later, the scent continues to weave its magic, funnelling over $3.3 million annually into Taylor's estate and her beloved AIDS charities. The magnitude of its success is simply breathtaking.

Her dalliances with billionaire magnate Malcolm Forbes and the dashing George Hamilton only added to her allure.

At the age of fifty-five, Elizabeth assumed the mantle of founder and chairperson for the American Foundation for AIDS Research (amfAR), alongside co-founder Mathilde Krim.

Every dollar raised since 1985 has been a beacon of hope, providing vital support to AIDS victims worldwide and disseminating crucial preventive information to the public. Elizabeth's unwavering commitment to this cause is nothing short of awe-inspiring, showcasing her enduring legacy as a humanitarian and advocate for change.

Elizabeth promotes her new fragrance, Passion, at Macy's San Francisco West, October 15, 1987

Elizabeth Taylor: My Celebrity Connection

In 1987, Elizabeth appeared on screen as Alice Moffit in the television movie "Poker Alice". It was a captivating spectacle; Elizabeth, more radiant than ever, effortlessly embodied the allure of a genuine Hollywood icon. It was as though she herself had emerged from a chrysalis unfolding her delicate wings and catching the first rays of dawn like a canvas touched by the morning light.

The appointment of renowned costume designer Nolan Miller only added to the anticipation, promising a visual feast for viewers.

Despite the passage of time, Elizabeth retained the captivating charm and magnetism that had made her a household name. With every glance and every line delivered on screen, she reaffirmed her status as a bona fide movie star, leaving audiences spellbound by her timeless appeal.

What truly distinguished Elizabeth's later on-screen appearances was her unwavering commitment to her philanthropic endeavours. In a remarkable display of generosity, she pledged to donate all earnings from her remaining acting roles to her AIDS charities. Sometimes, she would even agree to take on a role only if the proceeds were dedicated to her second passion in life—her enduring love for Richard Burton.

THE POKER ALICE-SCREEN-WORN SHOES

These shoes were made as part of a period gown for Elizabeth for her role in the TV movie, *Poker Alice*. The shoes are a size 8 and are pink satin. Each shoe has a beautiful flower that embellishes each toe. "E. T." is inscribed inside of each shoe.

The shoes were designed by Hollywood designer Nolan Miller. He was best known for his lavish, extravagant costumes and big-shouldered jackets and dresses for the 1980s drama TV shows, such as *Dynasty*.

Source: Heritage Auction House, Dallas, Texas/ Nolan Miller estate.

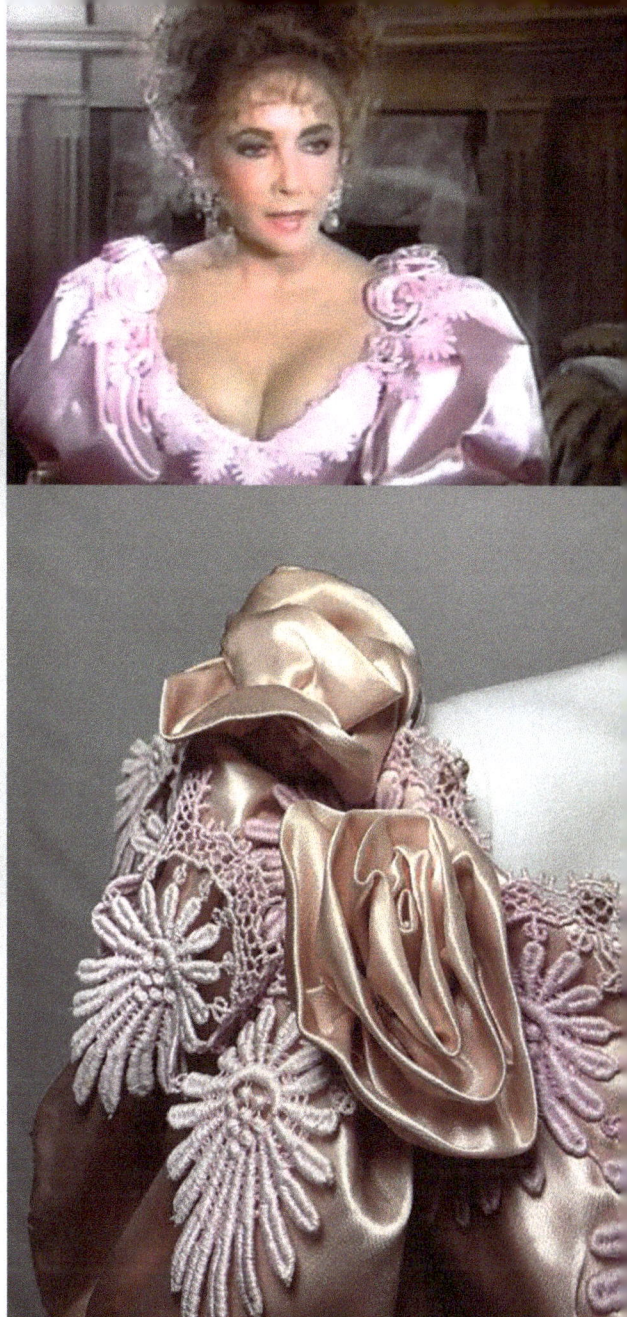

Elizabeth Taylor: My Celebrity Connection

258 | *Elizabeth Taylor: My Celebrity Connection*

"POKER ALICE"

TAFFETA MOIRÉ COMPLIMENTED WITH SILK FLOWERS

Another gown that was worn by Elizabeth in her role as Alice Moffit in the TV movie *Poker Alice*, also starring George Hamilton. The is a Nolan Miller four-piece deep-garnet moiré taffeta travel costume with matching hat. The jacket and skirt are taffeta moiré, satin, and cotton lace. The underskirt is taffeta. The hat is velvet, taffeta moiré complimented with silk flowers, feathers, and lace. The jacket and skirt are labelled Nolan Miller. Dress size is 4/6, and the hat has no size.

Source: Heritage Auction House, Dallas, Texas/ Nolan Miller estate.

Elizabeth Taylor: My Celebrity Connection

260 | *Elizabeth Taylor: My Celebrity Connection*

SIGNED ALICE FAUX PLAYING CARDS

Robert Sheldon, founder and long-time president of Old Tucson Studios, first met Elizabeth in the early 1960s. He shared the silver screen with Elizabeth in her role as Alice Moffit in *Poker Alice*, and after filming had ended, Elizabeth gave Robert this pack of cards with one signed as a memory of their time together on the set.

Source: Robert Sheldon/Old Tuscan Studio's/Elizabeth Taylor.

Elizabeth Taylor: My Celebrity Connection | 261

262 | *Elizabeth Taylor: My Celebrity Connection*

PERIWINKLE BLUE

Here is a third outfit from Nolan Miller. This periwinkle-blue embroidered wool-and-satin costume weighing 45 kilos and was worn on the set of the movie made for television.

Source: Antique Dress England/Nolan Miller.

Elizabeth Taylor: My Celebrity Connection

Amid her battle with back pain and the challenges of excessive alcohol and drug use, Elizabeth found herself returning to the renowned Betty Ford Centre on October 24, 1988, seeking solace for the second time. This pivotal juncture in her life was defined by profound vulnerability and the courageous pursuit of healing.

In the same year, I took the first step in reaching out to Elizabeth, sending a heartfelt "get well" card to her sanctuary at the Bob Hope Drive, Rancho Mirage estate, where she had taken refuge under the guise of Ruth Warner.

The mere act of reaching out was a testament to the deep admiration I held for her, and it opened the door to a remarkable celebrity connection.

Upon confirming Elizabeth's admission with the facility, I was met with warmth and gratitude by a compassionate staff member. Their appreciation for the gesture of flowers and the simple act of reaching out was humbling.

Little did I know, this brief exchange would lay the foundation for a remarkable pen-friend relationship that would endure for years to come.

From that moment onward, a bond formed between us, transcending the barriers of celebrity and fan.

Our correspondence became a source of solace and connection, spanning across years of highs and lows in both of our lives.

Even as Elizabeth's journey on this earth came to a close in 2011, the memories of our exchanges remained etched in my heart, a testament to the profound impact she had on those fortunate enough to know her, even from afar.

It's truly remarkable how Elizabeth embraced her time at the Betty Ford facility as an opportunity for profound self-reflection and transformation.

Emerging from her rehabilitation on January 20, 1989, she had not only confronted her addictions but also channelled her experiences into a literary masterpiece. The publication of her bestseller, "Elizabeth Takes Off," was nothing short of a triumph—a testament to her resilience and authenticity.

Through her book, Elizabeth courageously bared her soul to the world, offering a candid glimpse into the struggles and challenges she had faced.

In sharing her journey to reclaim her health and self-esteem, she shattered the illusion of Hollywood glamour, revealing her humanity and vulnerability. It was a bold declaration that even icons like Elizabeth Taylor were not immune to the pressures and pitfalls of fame.

Yet, Elizabeth found solace and newfound companionship. Emerging from the shadows of loneliness, she embarked on a new chapter of her life with Larry Fortensky, a construction worker who, like her, was navigating the journey of recovery.

This is the picture that was pinned into a get-well card and accompanied by a bouquet of flowers. It began my lifelong pen-friend relationship with Elizabeth (1989).

Source: Elizabeth Taylor/Image Unknown.

Compliments of ELIZABETH TAYLOR

Thank you for the beautiful card and gorgeous flowers!

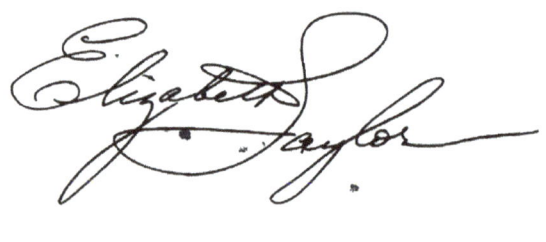

Have a Joyous Christmas, and a Wonderful New Year... All Year!

"Madonna"
Augustus John
From the Collection of
Miss Elizabeth Taylor

A Christmas card was soon to follow from Elizabeth to yours truly (1988).

Source: Elizabeth Taylor.

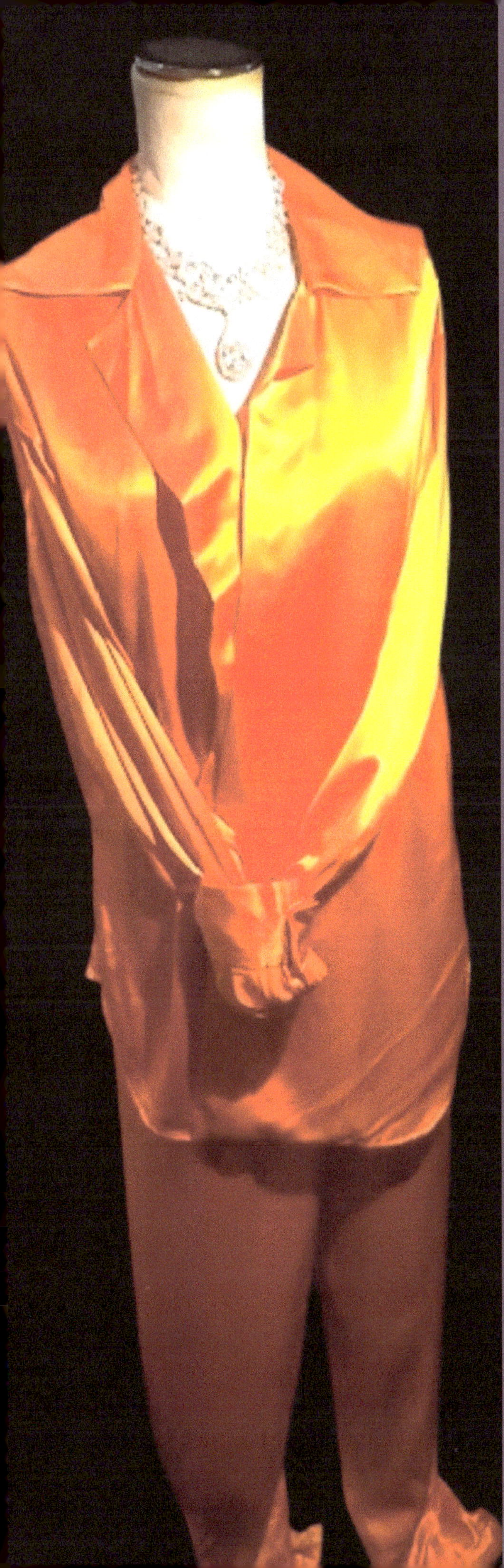

FASHION DESIGNER ANDRE VAN PIER

These beautiful orange satin pajamas were custom made for Elizabeth by famed designer Andre van Pier of Fifth Avenue. His creative influence is seen almost every day through television shows and commercials.

Fashion designer Andre van Pier died from a liver failure in the NYC Hospital in August of 2008 after a long battle with hepatitis-C.

Source: Gotta Have Rock and Roll Collectibles and Andre van Pier of Fifth Avenue.

MATILDA OTTO

This is a pear-shaped brooch with teardrop inset, adorned with Austrian crystals. This brooch once belonged to Elizabeth and was worn by her during a stage or movie production. After the event, Elizabeth gifted it to her longtime friend Matilda Otto.

Source: The Matilda Otto estate/ James McMahan from HeroProps4U.

Elizabeth arrives with new boyfriend,
Larry Fortensky, at the Los Angeles airport (1989).

Source: Bob Scott.

Elizabeth Taylor: My Celebrity Connection

*People have counted me down
and out too many times.
I'm a survivor
and proud of it.*
—Elizabeth Taylor

Despite her monumental achievements, her appearance at the "American Hope Awards" in March of 1989 painted a picture of struggle and resilience. Amidst the accolades and adoration, she bore the weight of her battles with a visible heaviness, a stark reminder of the human frailty that lurks beneath the veneer of fame.

The evening, a heartfelt tribute to Elizabeth's contributions to the silver screen and her relentless advocacy for AIDS awareness, was graced by the presence of her dear friend, Carol Burnett.

In a gesture of deep affection, Elizabeth presented Carol with a specially designed jacket—a token of their enduring friendship and shared experiences.

Despite the facade of happiness in her newfound romance, Elizabeth found herself ensnared once again by the spectre of alcohol and drug dependency.

A sinus infection and fever marked the beginning of a tumultuous chapter, leading to her admission to St. John's Hospital in Santa Monica on April 9, 1990. As weeks turned into agonising uncertainty, a lung biopsy revealed the ominous presence of pneumonia, plunging Elizabeth into a battle for her very survival.

At the brink of despair, Elizabeth's resilience shone through. Despite dire prognostications, she defied the odds, gradually stabilising under the watchful care of medical professionals.

Reports of her imminent demise on April 22 only served to underscore the magnitude of her struggle and the triumph of her spirit.

Emerging from her harrowing ordeal after a two-and-a-half-month hospital stay, Elizabeth's journey stood as a testament to the resilience of the human spirit, inspiring awe and admiration in all who bore witness to her indomitable will to live.

*I am finally glad to be going home.
My sole concern at this time is
focused on my getting well
and carrying on with my life.
—Elizabeth Taylor*

THE AMERICAN HOPE AWARDS

This dark-violet satin jacket was designed by and gifted from Elizabeth to Carol Burnett after she hosted the American Hope Awards in 1989. Elizabeth was the honoured guest and recipient of the American Hope Award during the all-star tribute. The front is embroidered with "Carol Burnett" in gold lettering. The back is embroidered with "Second Annual America's Hope Awards All-Star Tribute to Elizabeth Taylor."

Source: Celebrity Seconds, Palm Springs, California.

Elizabeth Taylor: My Celebrity Connection

Elizabeth, Larry Fortensky and Elizabeth's good friend, confidant and public-relations assistant Chen Sam arrive at the Los Angeles airport, where Elizabeth appeared in a Los Angeles court in a battle against ex-lover Henry Weinberg, who alleged that Passion, was a copy of a perfume he had developed and presented to Elizabeth but that she had sold it as her very own. Elizabeth was awarded an undisclosed amount.

Source: Bob Scott (1990).

The year 1991 Elizabeth Taylor found herself in the unforgiving spotlight of the courts.

This time, it was against a U.S. tabloid that dared to smear her name with sensationalised tales of her time at St. John's Hospital in Santa Monica, California, in April 1990. The audacious claims of alcohol binges and suicide watches, coupled with unfounded reports of lupus ravaging her iconic beauty, were nothing short of scandalous.

Yet, in the face of such baseless accusations, Elizabeth stood firm, unyielding in her pursuit of justice. With unwavering resolve, she embarked on yet another legal battle, emerging victorious and securing the settlement she rightfully deserved. The tabloids' penchant for sensationalism may have tried to tarnish her legacy, but Elizabeth's strength and fortitude shone through, a beacon of resilience in the face of adversity.

It's truly astounding how Elizabeth weathered such relentless scrutiny with grace and poise. Despite the loneliness that often accompanies such trials, she remained steadfast in her resolve, refusing to let the tabloids' malicious gossip dim her spirit. Her ability to rise above the fray, to navigate the stormy seas of fame with resilience and dignity, is a testament to her unwavering strength of character.

At the age of fifty-eight, Elizabeth emerged from the shadows of adversity with a newfound lease on life. With a new book in hand and a newfound love in the form of Larry Fortensky, a construction worker twenty years her junior whom she met during their time at the Betty Ford Centre.

Elizabeth embarked on a journey of renewal and rediscovery. Larry's presence grounded her, allowing her to revel in the simple joys of everyday life, from mundane tasks like supermarket shopping to the exhilarating embrace of newfound love.

*If all the public stopped
buying the nonsense,
then perhaps they would all
go out of business,
and wouldn't that just be so great.
—Elizabeth comments on tabloid press*

The romance between a construction worker and a Hollywood legend at the Betty Ford Centre captivated the world's imagination, weaving a tale of unexpected love amidst the trials of rehabilitation.

Surrounded by the tumult of tabloid headlines predicting their every move, Elizabeth and Larry's relationship weathered its fair share of ups and downs, with rumours swirling about their on-again, off-again status and the ever-shifting dynamics of their cohabitation.

But nothing could have prepared the world for the spectacle of their union—a wedding that would go down in history as the event of the year. Despite the passing decades and the trials she had faced, Elizabeth emerged radiant as ever, ready to embark on a new chapter of her life.

On October 6, 1991, she exchanged vows with Larry Fortensky, a man twenty years her junior, in a ceremony that captured the world's attention.

Draped in a breathtaking Valentino-designed wedding gown adorned with delicate lemon lace, Elizabeth exuded elegance and grace as she uttered the words "I do" for the eighth time.

The scene was set amongst an idyllic backdrop of Michael Jackson's Neverland Ranch, with an orchard-strewn summer gazebo serving as the altar for their million-dollar nuptials.

It was a moment of pure enchantment—a testament to love's enduring power to defy expectations and transcend boundaries.

*Well, I've been single for ten years.
I always thought—knowing my nature
as a marrying kind of woman—I would try
just one more time before I die.
—Elizabeth Taylor.*

Elizabeth was looking fabulous at an AIDS charity, just months after her eighth marriage to Larry Fortensky.

Source: Reed Cohn.

The momentous day of May 27, 1992, will forever be etched in my memory—it was the day I received a reply from Chen Sam, Elizabeth's trusted public-relations spokesperson of over two decades.

After years of tireless research and countless letters, I found myself on the brink of realising my dream of establishing a pen-pal relationship with the legendary Elizabeth Taylor. The journey to this point had been long and arduous, but now, standing on the precipice of possibility, I felt a surge of exhilaration unlike anything I had ever experienced.

In the realm of celebrity fandom, being a fan with a difference comes with its own set of challenges. Yet, with Elizabeth's attention finally within reach, I knew that the real work was just beginning.

Determined to nurture this newfound celebrity connection, I seized the opportunity to extend my well wishes to Elizabeth on her sixtieth birthday, sending a heartfelt card through Chen Sam in hopes of further solidifying our bond.

Meanwhile, Elizabeth wasted no time in leveraging her immense popularity to make a difference. Following the resounding success of her Passion fragrances, she unveiled yet another triumph in late 1992—the iconic White Diamonds fragrance.

Teaming up with Elizabeth Arden International, she embarked on a whirlwind tour to promote her fragrances and continue her tireless efforts in raising funds for AIDS charities.

Despite her absence from the silver screen for nearly five years, Elizabeth's presence remained palpable through her perfume advertisements and occasional appearances at AIDS charity events.

Her unwavering commitment to advocating for those affected by what was initially termed a "gay disease" persisted well into the late '90s and beyond, a testament to her boundless compassion and relentless pursuit of justice.

As the world would later bid farewell to this incomparable icon, Elizabeth's legacy of love, resilience, and activism continues to inspire generations to come.

THE BIRTHDAY NAPKIN

This lavender-coloured paper napkin was a part of the place settings for Elizabeth Taylor's sixtieth birthday. It is embellished in gold lettering with "Elizabeth's 60th Birthday." The napkin folds up 4 inches by 4 inches. Editor Michael Arlington was a special guest at the event and was quick to retrieve Elizabeth's used napkin from her place setting. Guests that attended the event were gifted with a tote bag that had a signed picture, feather mask, and birthday sweater enclosed.

Source: Magic Kingdom in Disneyland and guest Michael Arlington.

Elizabeth Taylor: My Celebrity Connection

Every guest who attended her sixtieth birthday bash at Disneyland received an especially designed sweater, tote bag, and autographed picture of Elizabeth with her Maltese terrier, Sugar. Elizabeth kindly sent me the gifts to add to my collection in 1992.

Source: Disneyland/Elizabeth Taylor.

284 | *Elizabeth Taylor: My Celebrity Connection*

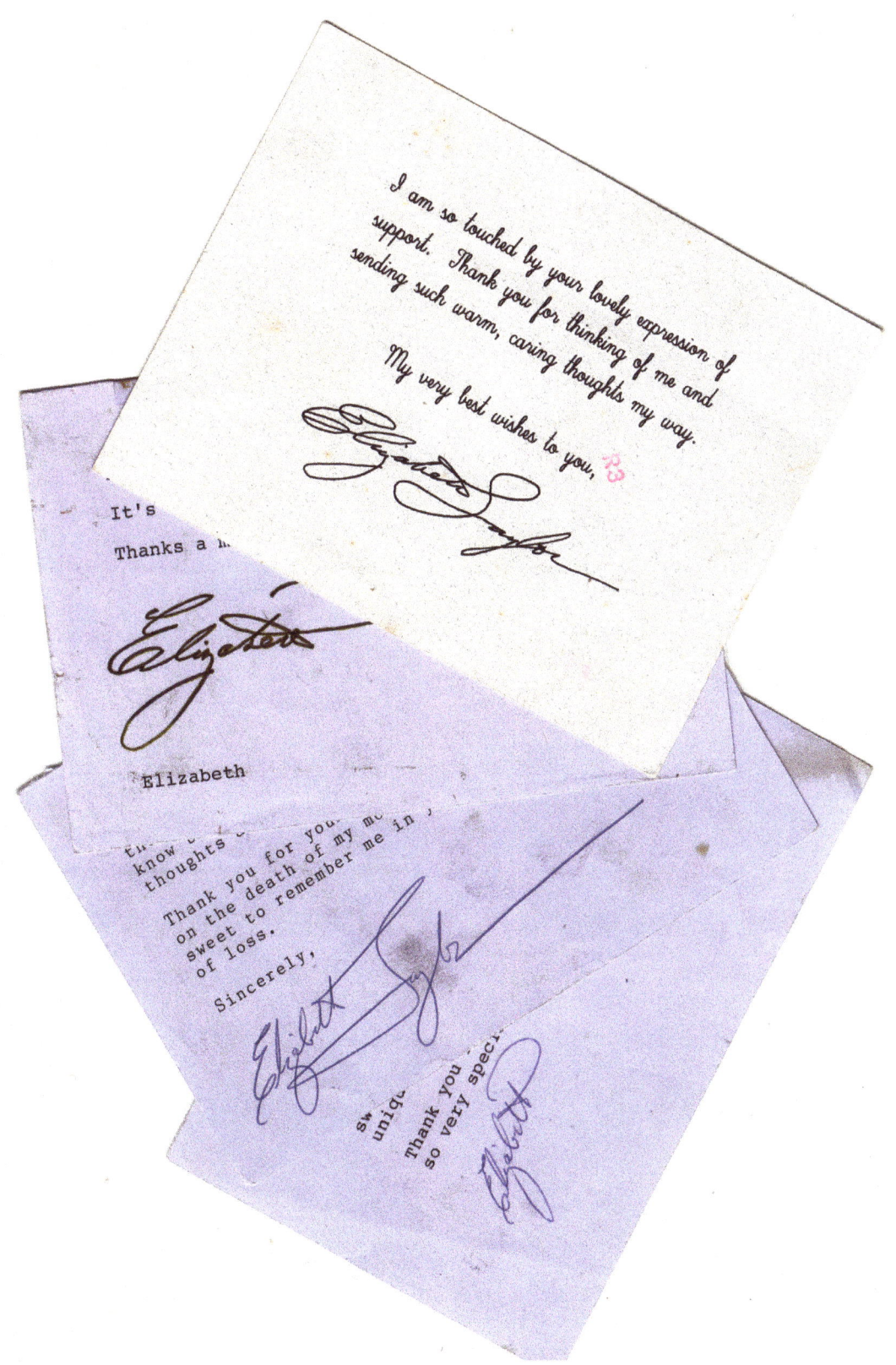

Elizabeth and Chen Sam kept up their correspondence and celebrity connection throughout the mid-1990s.

Source: Elizabeth Taylor/Chen Sam Associates (1992).

RHINESTONE ENCRUSTED

These boots are knee-high black suede, adorned with five bands of rhinestone. The toes are encrusted with ten rows of rhinestones, that is over 140 sparkling delights. A size 6, these boots show signs of wear. These boots were said to have been designed and gifted by Casadei of Italy for Elizabeth's sixtieth birthday. This pair of boots were later gifted to Elliot Goodwin of Larry's Shoe Museum, Texas, and then later sold to Stars Boutique. Founder of Stars Boutique, Lita Sahakian, is pictured with Hollywood designer Nolan Miller.

Source: Elliot Goodwin of Larry's Shoe Museum and Stars Boutique by Lita & Co.

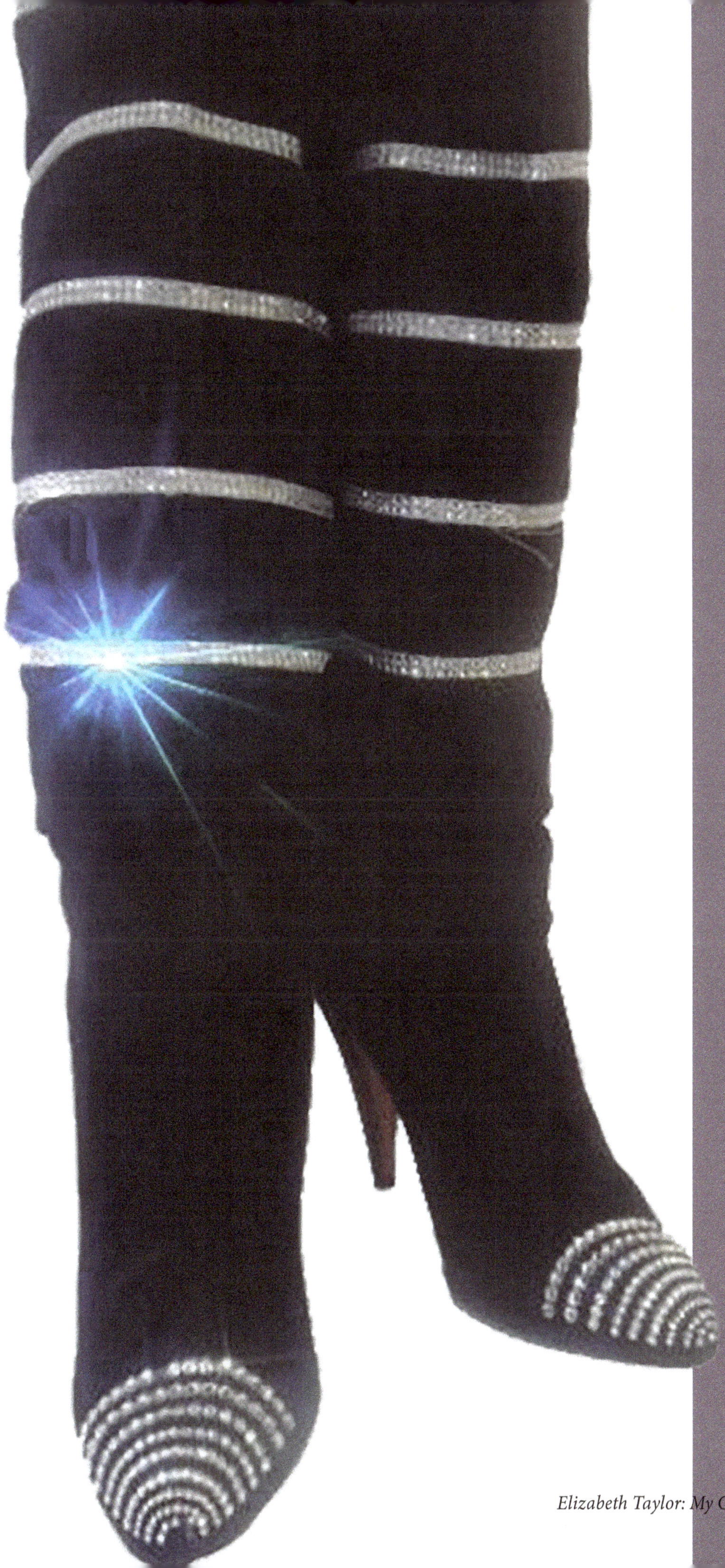

Elizabeth Taylor: My Celebrity Connection | 287

A PERSONAL GIFT FROM ELIZABETH

A portfolio of Elizabeth's release of White Diamonds in Australia 1991 was presented to Elizabeth and her public-relations council. Elizabeth wrote back and presented her no. 1 fan with a limited-edition (3000) signed perfume bottle and a wonderful letter.

Source: Elizabeth Taylor

Dear Wayne,

Chen Sam forwarded copies of your letters and the photographs to my home in California.

Thank you so much for being so thoughtful. I am told by my colleagues at the perfume company that the launch of White Diamonds went extremely well. I was so excited to get this news, followed by your kind letters.

I have spoken to our marketing department to see if they can assist you in obtaining a special edition bottle, and I am sure that you will be hearing from them shortly.

Hopefully one of these days I will get to Australia.

Affectionately,

Elizabeth

Elizabeth Taylor Fortensky

Confirmation from Elizabeth that I was indeed her no. 1 fan (1993).

Source: Elizabeth Taylor/ Herb Ritts.

On many occasions, Elizabeth was unable to respond personally. Quite often, I would receive autopen autographs. This is an original autopen autograph that I sent back to her and requested a handwritten autograph. It demonstrates the comparison between autopen and hand-signed autographs.

SANTA MONICA

This wonderful gold long-sleeved lama-lace top was worn by Elizabeth to a public event on October 9, 1992. The sleeves end in flared cuffs, and the top is lined with black silk chiffon.

It was made by Nolan Miller, who was one of Elizabeth's favourite fashion designers at the time.

Here you can see Elizabeth in the top, which was later acquired from Juliens Auctions, California.

Elizabeth and beloved pooch Sugar on her *White Diamonds* promotional tour, 1993.

Source: Jay Nass.

CHEN SAM & ASSOCIATES INC.

May 27, 1992

Dear Wayne,

It is always a pleasure to hear from you. You are truly Miss Taylor's #1 fan in Australia.

Miss Taylor will not be in Australia this year. In fact, in September she will most probably be touring in different cities in America in connection with her Aids projects.

Lots of luck, and thanks for the many letters you have sent to this office.

Best regards,

Chen Sam
Public Relations Counsel
to Elizabeth Taylor

cc: Joe Spellman   Tom Moloney
    Kim Coston   Carole Krisulevicz
    Michael Brillhart   Barbara Panetta

CS/ib

315 EAST 72ND STREET NEW YORK, NEW YORK 10021-4625
212 628 5915/9 FAX 212 439 9438

The many faces of Elizabeth Taylor as she promotes her fragrances at Parma Town USA, (1993).

The 1990s were my most prolific corresponding years with Elizabeth, but with her work schedule sometimes quite hectic, it was not always possible to correspond with her the way that a fan would perhaps like. However, Elizabeth's loyalty to her adoring public was evident on many levels, and quite often there would be times that items or questions would be returned unanswered because of her unavailability to personally respond. I grew to understand celebrity protocol and continued my celebrity connection.

In 1992, Elizabeth also reconnected with former Cat on a Hot Tin Roof co-star, Paul Newman, to present the Oscar nominees and awards. Elizabeth appeared looking as radiant as ever, with Paul Newman still his handsome self.

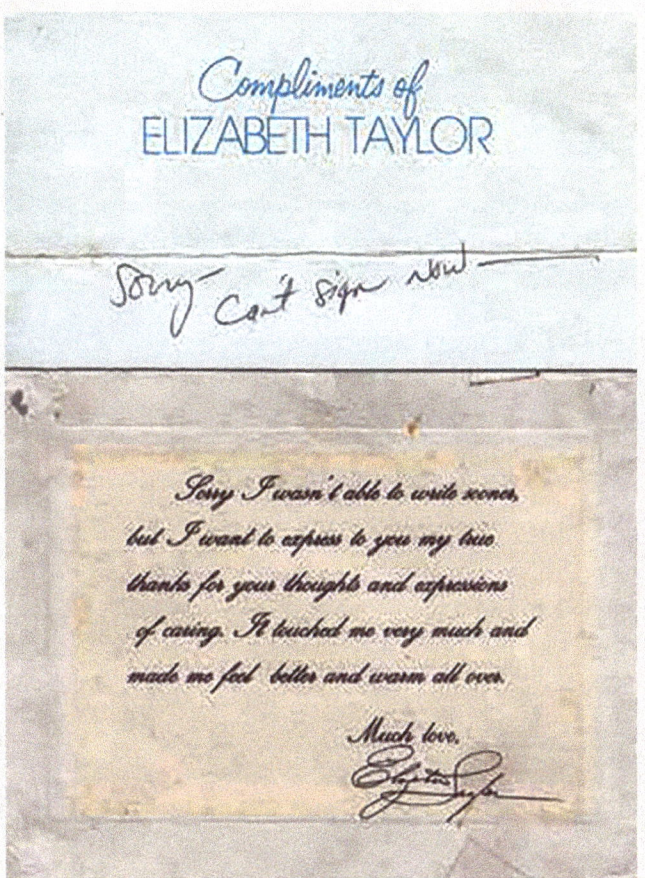

Dear Wayne:

Thank you for your lovely photo book paying tribute to Miss Taylor. It is very kind of you to take the time to write and share these pictures with her.

Thank you for your friendship and support. Best wishes to you today and always.

Sincerely,

Sharon

Sharon Leigh

Dear Wayne,

I am happy to know that things are much better with you now. I hope that it will continue for a long, long time.

In answer to your question about Elizabeth, she will not be going to Australia until 1994.

Thanks for being such a loyal fan.

Sincerely,

Chen

Chen Sam
Public Relations Counsel
to Elizabeth Taylor Fortensky

Dear Wayne:

Thank you for the beautiful (and gigantic!) Christmas cards, which we all very much enjoyed receiving. They are really lovely and certainly brightened our holiday season.

Best wishes to you for a bright and happy New Year.

Sincerely,

SLeigh

Sharon Leigh

Dear Wayne,

We are in receipt of your cards to Elizabeth Taylor and want you to know we are sending them directly to her.

Thanks you for your thoughtfulness and good luck on your new move and future endeavors.

Sincerely,

Chen Sam

ELIZABETH TAYLOR

After battling yet another severe respiratory infection that had kept her bedridden since November 1992, Elizabeth emerged with breathtaking resilience, defying all odds to make a triumphant return to the public eye.

With unwavering determination, she embarked on a courageous journey to attend her dear friend Michael Jackson's grand soirée at the American Music Awards, refusing to let illness dampen her indomitable spirit.

In a moment of pure astonishment, Elizabeth was bestowed with the prestigious Jean Hersholt Humanitarian Award in the latter part of 1993—a testament to her unwavering commitment to making a difference in the world. Her tireless efforts in championing humanitarian causes left audiences spellbound, as she stood as a beacon of hope and compassion in a world often fraught with adversity.

But Elizabeth's trailblazing spirit didn't stop there. In a dazzling display of creativity and innovation, she unveiled the follow-up to her iconic White Diamonds fragrance—the enchanting Diamond and Rubies, Emeralds, and Sapphires collection. With each scent embodying the allure of precious gemstones, Elizabeth once again captivated hearts and minds, leaving an indelible mark on the world of fragrance.

As she continued to defy expectations and push boundaries, Elizabeth's legacy of resilience and compassion continued to inspire generations to come. Her unwavering commitment to making a difference, both on and off the screen, served as a powerful reminder of the transformative power of love and hope.

Source: Sam Emerson.

With the sorrowful news of her mother's passing at the age of eighty-two weighing heavily on her heart in 1994, Elizabeth's resilience was put to the ultimate test. Coupled with the daunting task of recovering from a hip operation, she faced the daunting prospect of an extended period of bed rest and the need to shed 20 kilos before undergoing her second hip replacement later in the year.

Despite the shadows that loomed over her, Elizabeth's unwavering spirit shone through as she embarked on a remarkable journey of creativity and innovation. Teaming up with Avon, she poured her heart and soul into the creation of the Avon-Taylor jewellery line—a testament to her enduring legacy as a household name.

Her fragrances had long inspired millions, and now, with her new line of jewellery, she was poised to expand the Taylor empire, bringing a touch of elegance and sophistication into the lives of everyday American women. Collaborating with the talented Katherine Ireland, Elizabeth curated a stunning collection of jewellery that captured the essence of her timeless charm and grace.

Following a full recovery from her hip surgery, Elizabeth made a triumphant return to the silver screen with a brief cameo appearance in Steven Spielberg's blockbuster film, "The Flintstones." Her decision to take on the role was fuelled by her unwavering commitment to her AIDS charities, with the entirety of her $2.5 million fee pledged to support their noble cause.

It was a joyous moment to witness Elizabeth reclaiming her rightful place on the big screen, radiating with all the brilliance and charisma that had made her a beloved icon for generations.

In yet another remarkable gesture of generosity, Elizabeth lent her voice to "The Simpsons" character Maggie in 1994, marking a memorable milestone in her illustrious career.

Her contribution, though seemingly simple, spoke volumes about her compassionate spirit, with the entirety of her $1 million fee donated to charitable causes.

ELIZABETH'S FABULOUS SWEATER

Elizabeth's journey with Larry brought her to a place she had never imagined—a life away from the glaring spotlight that had defined her existence as a celebrity. Together, they ventured into the ordinary realm of everyday life, embarking on simple outings like shopping at the supermarket.

For Elizabeth, these seemingly mundane activities took on a whole new significance, as she marvelled at experiences she had never before encountered.

Elizabeth Taylor: My Celebrity Connection

In the aisles of the supermarket, Elizabeth found a newfound sense of freedom and joy—a departure from the relentless scrutiny of her celebrity persona. It was a revelation that brought her true contentment, a solace that transcended the allure of any movie role she had ever played.

For the first time in ages, Elizabeth embraced her true self with a sense of ease and authenticity, revelling in the simplicity of ordinary life.

One treasure from this newfound happiness was a woollen-blend cashmere sweater—a vibrant homage to Gustav Klimt's iconic painting.

Adorned with colourful depictions, this sweater became a symbol of Elizabeth's newfound sense of self and contentment. In a rare glimpse into her private life, she wore this sweater for a magazine shoot, inviting readers into her world alongside Larry, where happiness radiated from every corner.

*I feel my body and my spirits
growing stronger;
I look forward to being more active
and to following my great sense of adventure
and basically getting back to my world travels.
—Elizabeth Taylor*

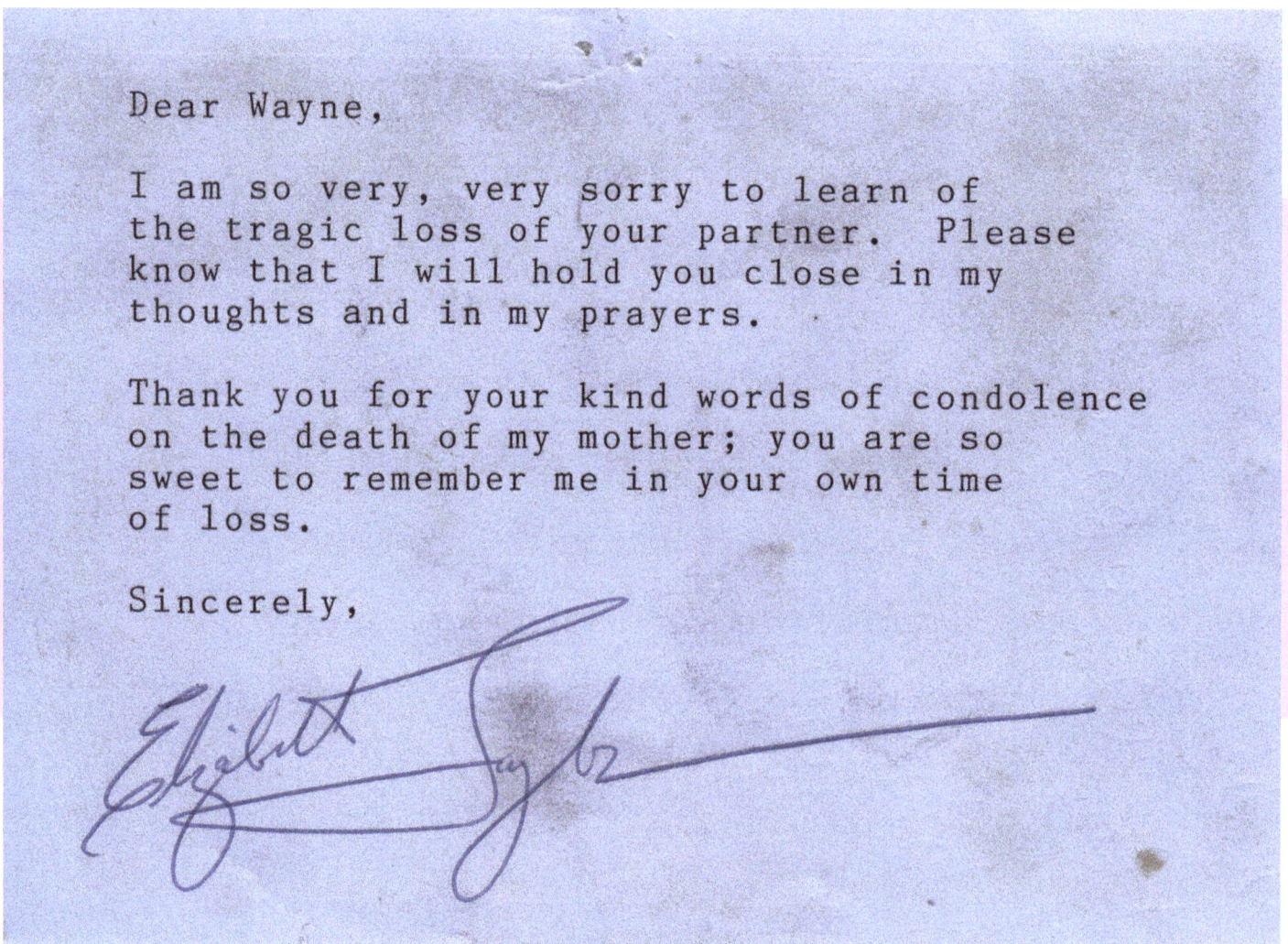

Elizabeth was so very lovely to send her condolences on the death of my partner in 1994.

Source: Elizabeth Taylor.

Original promotional shoot for
the newly launched Avon jewelry line in 1994.

Source: Visage Images.

From the Elizabeth Taylor jewelry collections came such pieces as the passion flower collection; the purple iridescent glass necklace; the elephant walk brooch and the amethyst encrusted ring.

Source: Visage Images.

306 | *Elizabeth Taylor: My Celebrity Connection*

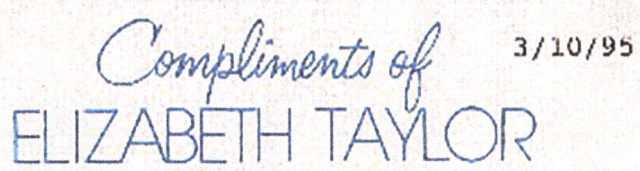

In this card from Sharon Leigh (fan mail secretary) dated October 3, 1995, I am informed that Elizabeth is currently unavailable to provide the personalised autograph I am seeking. An alternative was provided.

308 | *Elizabeth Taylor: My Celebrity Connection*

THE LAVENDER SATIN-AND-RHINESTONE CLUTCH

Back in the '80s, co-founder of Star Wares, Marcia Tysseling, appeared as an extra on the show *Murphy Brown*. Elizabeth happens to be the guest star of the show that day and her assistant Tim, just happened to be an old friend of Melissa Rivers.

Marcia hooked up with Tim and Elizabeth invited Marcia to her home to collect several items she was willing to donate for charity. Usually, the items received from Elizabeth were shoes and, oddly enough, vases and baskets.

When contacting Marcia, she said, "I honestly don't think she wanted her clothing sold based on insecurity of her current weight. I can totally relate and respect that. Didn't matter…I was just happy to have her as one of my consignors."

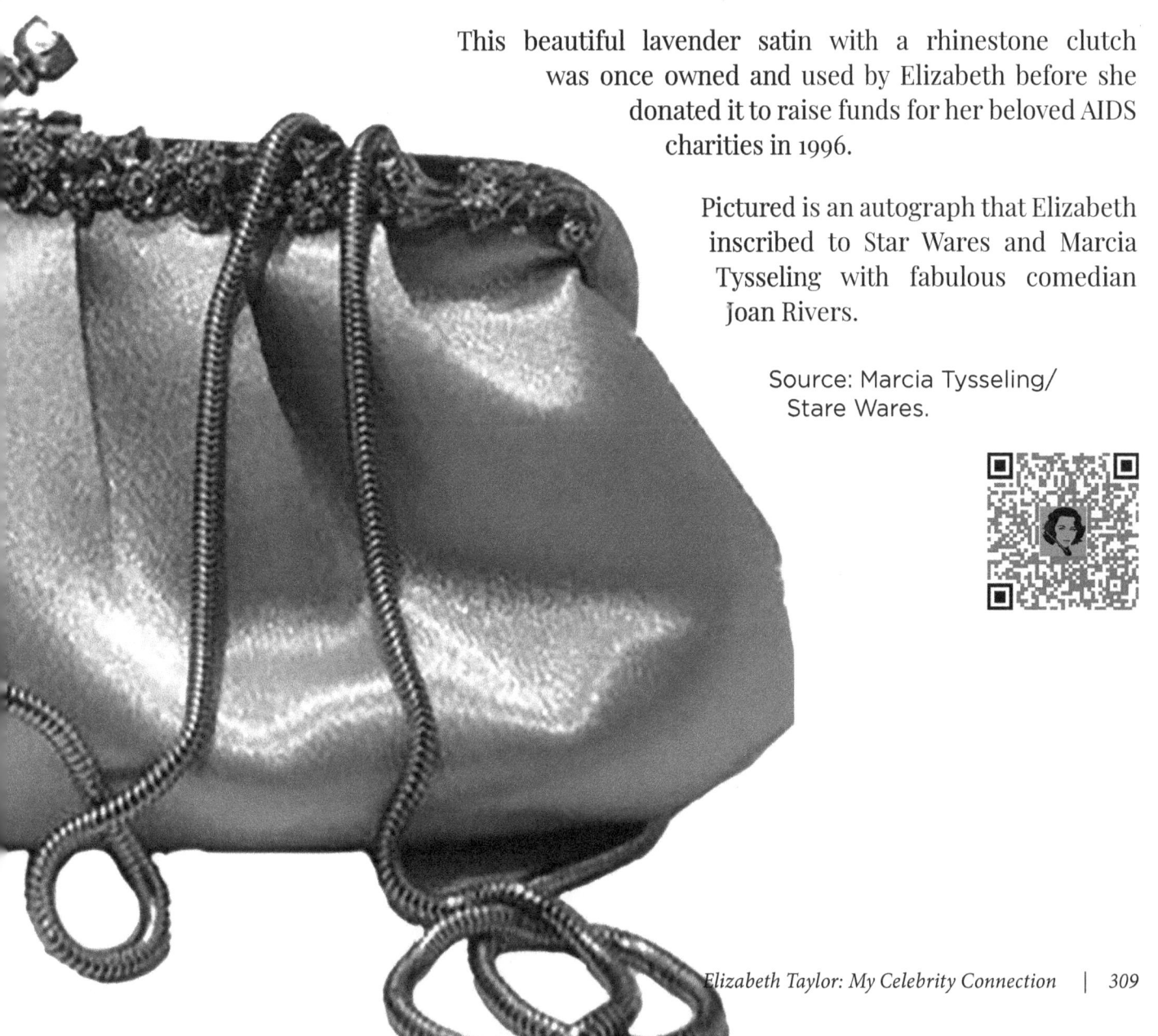

This beautiful lavender satin with a rhinestone clutch was once owned and used by Elizabeth before she donated it to raise funds for her beloved AIDS charities in 1996.

Pictured is an autograph that Elizabeth inscribed to Star Wares and Marcia Tysseling with fabulous comedian Joan Rivers.

Source: Marcia Tysseling/Stare Wares.

In early 1996, Elizabeth Taylor embarked on yet another exhilarating journey with the release of her latest fragrance, Black Pearls. Bursting with floral notes intertwined with spices and sandalwood, this enchanting scent quickly captured the hearts of fragrance enthusiasts worldwide.

With its captivating allure, Black Pearls soared to unprecedented heights, cementing its place as one of Elizabeth's most beloved fragrances.

In a stroke of brilliance, Elizabeth leveraged the popularity of Black Pearls to embark on a whimsical adventure across four CBS sitcoms. A lucrative deal worth $250,000 saw her making guest appearances, weaving a delightful tale centred around a captivating black-pearl necklace that seemed to have a mind of its own, getting lost or stolen from show to show.

It was a mesmerising journey that showcased Elizabeth's boundless creativity and flair for storytelling, captivating audiences with each whimsical twist and turn.

Despite her best efforts, her marriage to Larry Fortensky began to unravel, culminating in a bittersweet divorce on October 31, 1996—the eighth and final chapter in Elizabeth's storied romantic history.

Even in the face of adversity, Elizabeth's indomitable spirit shone through as she redirected her focus to her lifelong passion: AIDS advocacy.

Undeterred by the challenges she faced, Elizabeth forged ahead with unwavering determination, channelling her energy into the formation of the Elizabeth Taylor AIDS Foundation.

With renewed purpose, she embarked on a mission to combat the devastating impact of the disease, using her platform to raise awareness and enact meaningful change.

In a testament to her resilience and dedication, Elizabeth seized every opportunity to champion her cause, even using her appearance on the hit sitcom "The Nanny" as a platform to promote her new fragrance, Black Pearls.

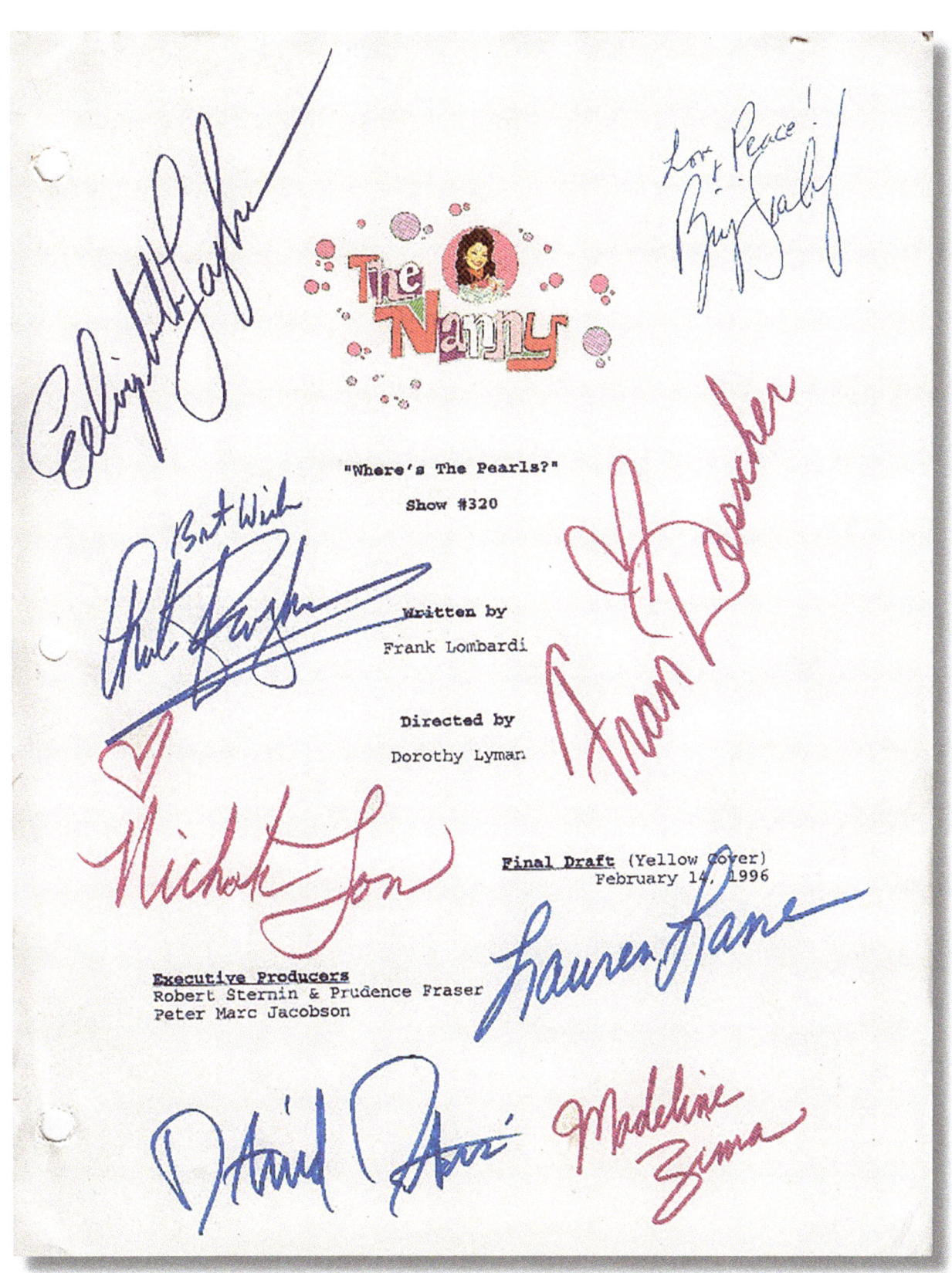

This original script for the Nanny episode "Where's the Pearls?", is signed by all cast members including Elizabeth Taylor, February 14, 1996.

Elizabeth Taylor: My Celebrity Connection

A DREAM COME TRUE

This pair of black-and-gold-embossed, open-toed, ankle-strapped, gold-braided Margaret J. shoes were also part of the items Elizabeth donated from her personal wardrobe. The shoes are a size 6B. A celebrity connection can come in all shapes and sizes and to know that these shoes came from Elizabeth's very own wardrobe—and I now owned them—was something that I had only dreamed about so many years ago. Let's face it, who doesn't want a pair of shoes worn by their favourite celebrity?

Source: Star Wares Collectables, California.

THE VIOLET AND PINK BELTS

On another consignment Elizabeth donated two belts, which were part of a list of many items that include hair wraps, bandanas, and scarves that were donated to benefit the Elizabeth Taylor AIDS Foundation. Both belts are made by Italian designer Vaneli Vero Curio.

The first belt is leather and has been dyed pink, and the second is made of leather with a lavender satin lining. The diameter of both belts is 14 inches. Elizabeth is pictured here wearing a similar, if not the same, pink belt.

Source: Star Wares on Main, Santa Monica, California.

Elizabeth Taylor: My Celebrity Connection

I just don't want to do it; it would injure my sense of privacy and would hurt people who are really well known.
—Elizabeth Taylor talking about her possible autobiography

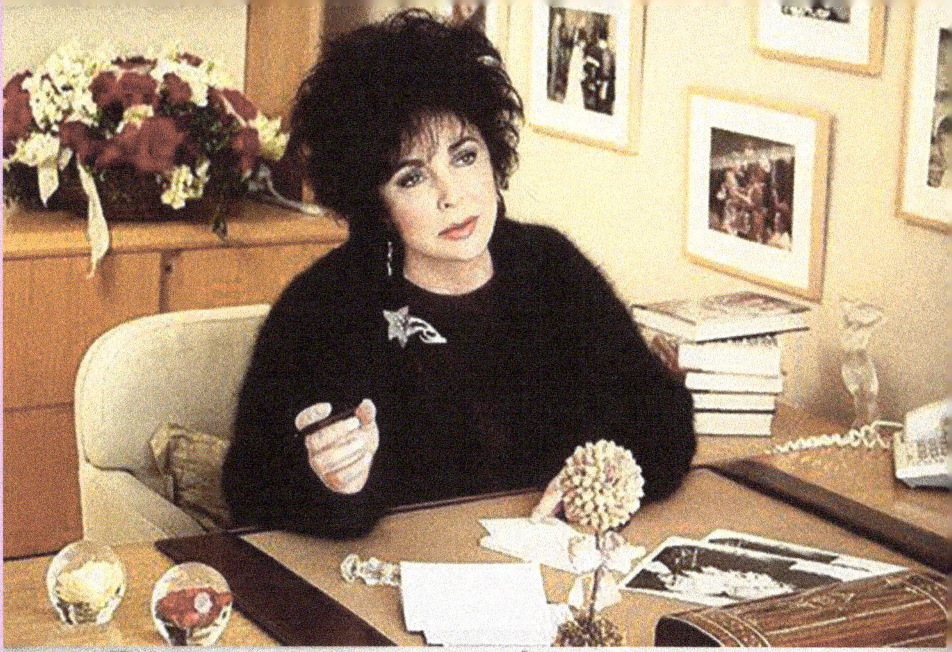

HAPPY BIRTHDAY

In 1996, I wrote to Elizabeth and informed her that whilst we had been in past correspondence, no one believed me. No one believed that I had developed a pen-friendship with the queen of Hollywood. Elizabeth took on this challenge and sent through a personal birthday greeting. One presumes she had just gone to the stationary drawer, found this Vincent van Gogh card, and had her executive secretary, Geoff Blain, send it.

Source: Elizabeth Taylor.

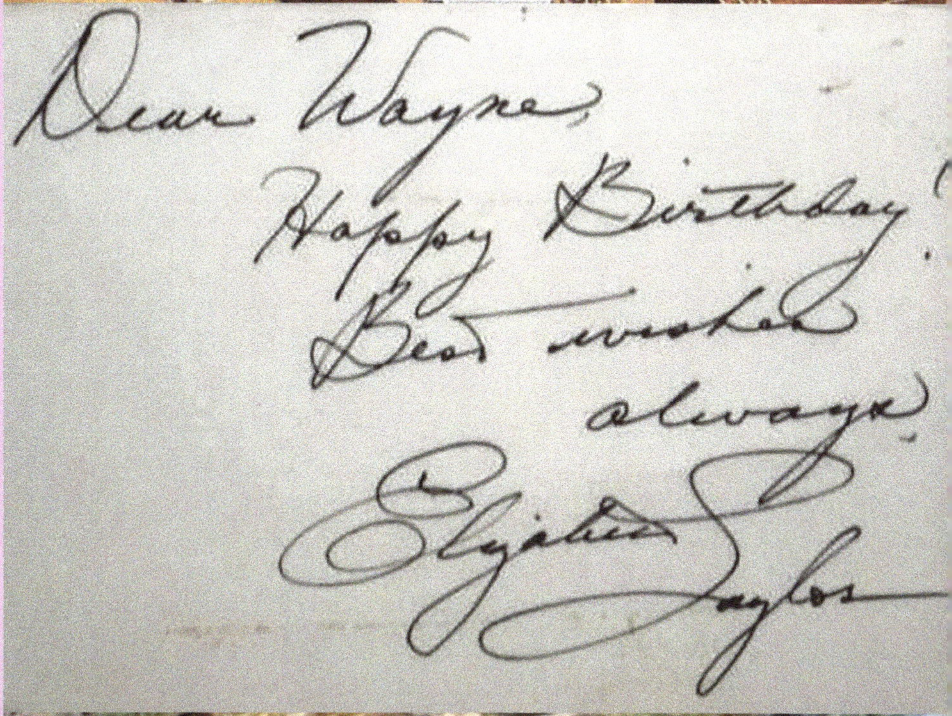

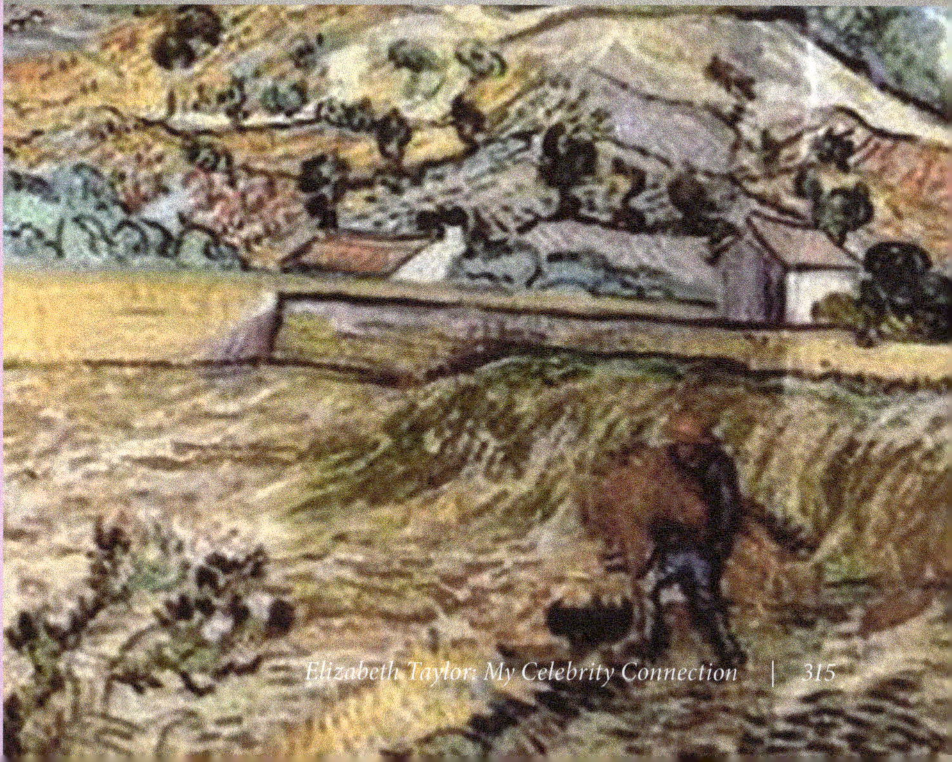

ELIZABETH EMMANUEL

This two-piece cotton cream skirt and jacket is complemented by dark-blue stripes around the wrist and above the jacket hem. The jacket has welt pockets and five self-covered buttons. This item was created by British designers Elizabeth and David Emanuel. It was acquired from the personal wardrobe of Elizabeth Taylor by Melissa Rivers for an animal-shelter fundraising event.

Source; Star Wares on Main, Santa Monica, California.

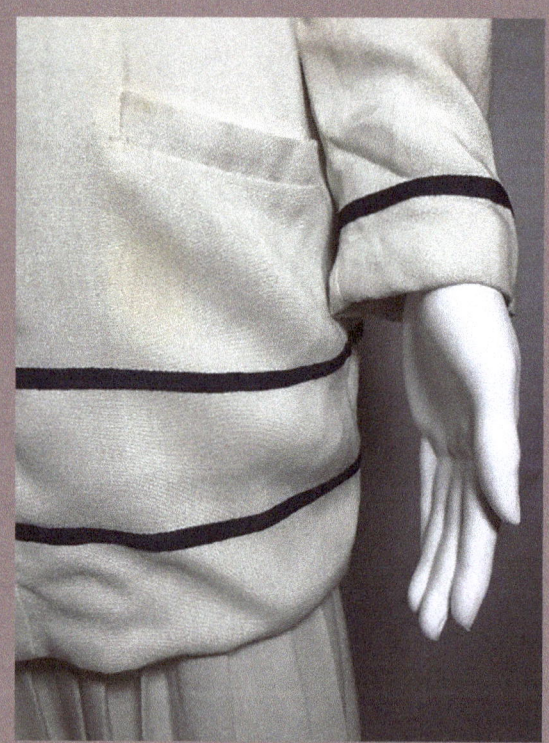

August 26, 1996, Elizabeth bid farewell to her dear friend and trusted confidant, Chen Sam. After a courageous battle with breast cancer, Chen Sam's untimely passing left a void in Elizabeth's world—a testament to the profound impact of their enduring friendship.

For over twenty-two years, Chen Sam had been a steadfast presence in Elizabeth's life, serving as both a loyal companion and dedicated public relations counsel.

Through countless interactions, he had become a familiar face to admirers like myself, entrusted with the task of delivering our tokens of affection to Elizabeth's doorstep.

As a reminder of their cherished bond, Elizabeth is captured here in a timeless photograph alongside Chen Sam, attending the 16th Annual Fragrance Foundation Recognition Awards at the prestigious Waldorf Hotel in New York City.

Their enduring friendship and shared moments of triumph and celebration serve as a testament to the power of genuine connection and the profound impact of loyalty and camaraderie.

Source: Bob Scott.

*Chen Sam became like a sister,
the sweetest woman in the world.
— Elizabeth Taylor*

On February 15, 1997, a spectacular moment unfolded as Elizabeth Taylor graced the illustrious stage of the Pantages Theatre. To the delight of the audience, she was elegantly escorted by her longtime friend, the iconic Michael Jackson, creating a scene of unparalleled panache and allure.

The air was electric with anticipation as the black-tie benefit, "Happy Birthday Elizabeth: A Celebration of Life," commenced—a remarkable occasion that transcended mere festivities to raise over $1.3 million for the Elizabeth AIDS Foundation.

As if touched by the hand of fate, Hollywood Boulevard itself bore witness to Elizabeth's unparalleled legacy, with a stretch of its famed pavement renamed "Elizabeth Way" in honor of her remarkable achievements and her sixty-fifth birthday celebration. It was a fitting tribute to a woman whose influence extended far beyond the silver screen, leaving an indelible mark on the hearts of countless admirers.

Following her birthday celebration, Elizabeth found herself admitted to the renowned Cedars Sinai Medical Centre in Los Angeles, where she underwent a gruelling four-hour operation to remove a 5-centimeter brain tumour—a silent adversary that had plagued her with debilitating headaches and dizziness in the preceding weeks.

In a cruel twist of fate, it was also revealed that Elizabeth had been diagnosed with diabetes, adding another layer of complexity to her already formidable health challenges.

Throughout her ordeal, Elizabeth was surrounded by an outpouring of love and support from family, friends, and admirers alike, their unwavering presence a testament to the profound impact she had on their lives.

Surrounded by a sea of floral tributes and well wishes, Elizabeth humbly requested that instead of sending flowers or cards, donations to her AIDS foundation would be greatly appreciated—a poignant reminder of her unwavering commitment to making a difference in the lives of those affected by the disease.

Today, Elizabeth's journey serves as a beacon of hope and inspiration to all who have had the privilege of witnessing her extraordinary life unfold.

Source: Herb Ritts/Elizabeth Taylor.

In a captivating display of resilience, Elizabeth Taylor emerged into the public eye once more, radiating health, happiness, and undeniable charm with her stunning silver hair.

At an AIDS benefit in San Francisco, she captivated audiences with her presence, delivering a speech that moved hearts and minds alike—a poignant tribute to the legacies of the late Princess Diana and Mother Teresa.

Caught in a moment of grace and elegance, Elizabeth graced a reception at Christie's Auction House in New York on March 16, 1999.

Her regal demeanour and timeless beauty left onlookers mesmerized, a testament to her enduring allure and timeless appeal.

However, just as the world began to celebrate her triumphant return, fate dealt Elizabeth another unexpected blow. Less than a year after undergoing surgery to remove a brain tumour, she found herself battling yet another mystery illness—a debilitating spinal fracture that threatened to derail her remarkable journey of resilience and perseverance.

On May 16, 2000, she took centre stage at Buckingham Palace for a momentous audience with Queen Elizabeth II—a historic occasion where she was officially bestowed the title of dame commander of the Order of the British Empire. Stepping forward with grace and dignity, Elizabeth stood before the queen, her famous Taylor diamond sparkling in the light—a symbol of her unwavering commitment to acting and charity alike.

Despite the challenges posed by ongoing hip and back problems, Elizabeth's determination to fulfill her duties knew no bounds. Alongside 143 other honourees, including the illustrious Julie Andrews, she stood tall, a beacon of strength and inspiration for all.

Source: Reed Cohn.

To celebrate the fact that Elizabeth was made a dame on my birthday, May 16, she sent me an updated autograph.

Source: Ralph Merlino.

*Me a dame...
a dameship,
this is the most exciting—
and I do not exaggerate—
day of my life.
—Elizabeth Taylor*

ELIZABETH HAS A FANCY TUNIC

Elizabeth wore this fancy tunic to a public event in 2000. It is a black sheer netting entirely covered with multicoloured ornate sequins and beads. The tunic has no label but is an amazement of detailed embossment. Elizabeth is pictured here wearing the tunic, which was later acquired from Julien's Auctions, California, at the "Lifestyle of Elizabeth Taylor" auction.

RHINESTONE CHECKERS

Reminiscent of the 1940s animal patch, this is an adorable midnight-blue faux-fur clutch with an overlay of rhinestone mesh in a checkerboard pattern. Elizabeth used this very clutch when attending an AIDS charity with Elton John and the Osbornes in 2000.

Source: Getty Images and Julien's Auctions, California.

Elizabeth appeared as a special guest
at her friend Michael Jackson's family
honour celebrations at Madison Square Garden,
New York, September 10, 2001.

Source: Reed Cohn.

In 2001, Elizabeth continued her remarkable journey on the celebrity-perfume frontier, unveiling yet another olfactory masterpiece infused with her signature style.

With a blend of carnation, Bulgarian rose, and mandarin orange, "Sparkling Diamonds" captivated hearts and senses alike, solidifying Elizabeth's status as a true fragrance icon.

A grand musical celebration in her honour took centre stage at the illustrious Royal Albert Hall in England on May 26, 2001—a momentous occasion that paid homage to Elizabeth's enduring legacy as a cinematic legend.

But the excitement didn't end there. In October of the same year, Elizabeth joined forces with fellow Hollywood sirens Joan Collins, Debbie Reynolds, and Shirley MacLaine in a star-studded TV film comedy slated for release in early 2002.

"These Old Broads," penned by Debbie Reynolds's daughter, Carrie Fisher, unfolded the tale of three aging divas reluctantly reuniting to create a TV series—an enchanting narrative that brought together legends of the silver screen in a celebration of timeless talent.

The reunion of Elizabeth and Debbie Reynolds, once linked by the ties of matrimony to the same man, was a poignant reminder of the passage of time and the power of forgiveness. Their collaboration in "These Old Broads" symbolised a reconciliation that transcended the scars of the past, showcasing a newfound harmony and mutual respect between two iconic figures.

Despite grappling with health challenges, Elizabeth's unwavering commitment to philanthropy remained steadfast. By the end

of 2001, her tireless efforts had raised an astonishing $600 million for AIDS research—a testament to her enduring dedication to making a difference in the lives of those affected by the disease.

Elizabeth still found time to nurture her bond with her number one fan—a touching reminder of the enduring connection that spanned decades and touched hearts in ways that words alone could never express.

Source: Reed Cohn.

Beautiful image of Elizabeth signed in silver pen.

Source: Elizabeth Taylor/ Bruce Weber.

Elizabeth Taylor: My Celebrity Connection | 327

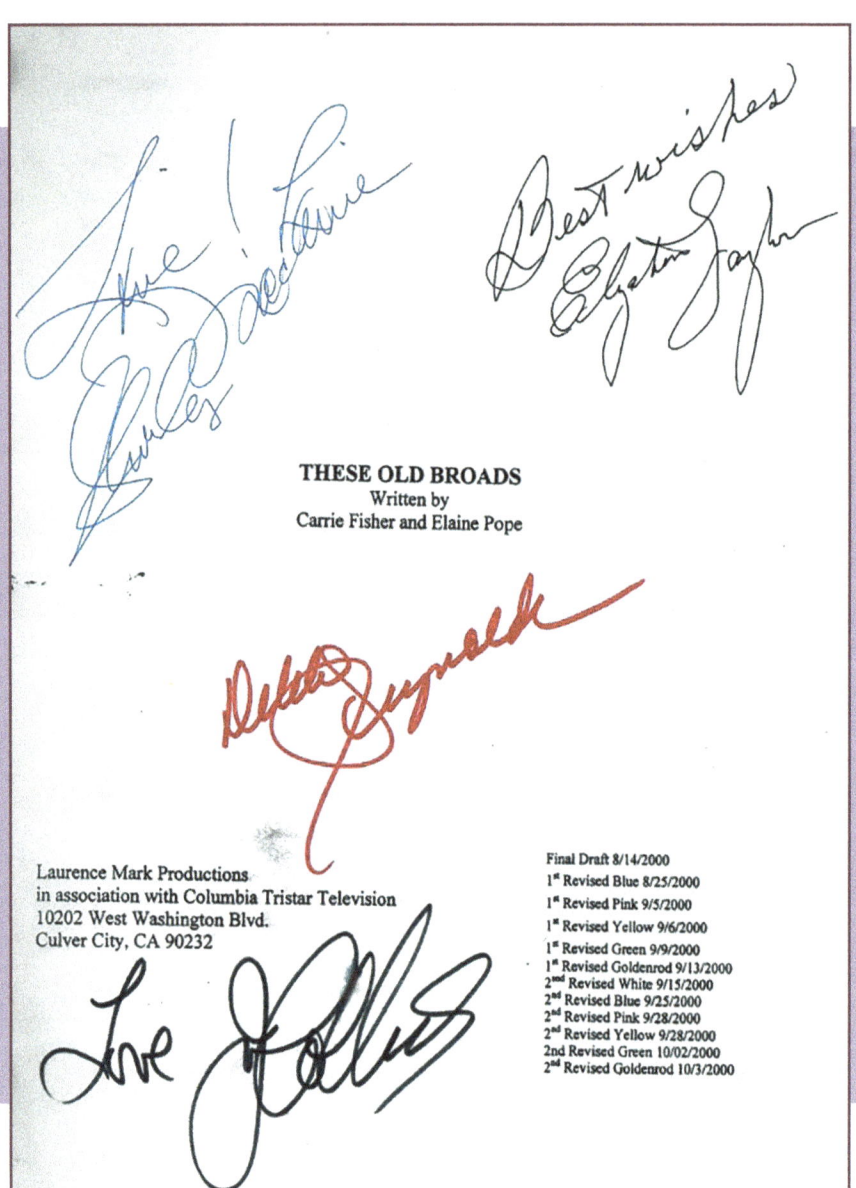

THESE OLD BROADS

Whilst filming the dance number between takes, Paul Keylock got a copy of the script and asked the ladies cheekily if they could sign it undedicated.

They were all darlings, so Paul felt comfortable asking. The front page is signed in a variety of colours by the four leading ladies. Paul Keylock was the personal assistant to Joan Collins on the set of *These Old Broads*.

The script was written by the late Carrie Fisher.

Source: Paul Keylock

Despite her physical limitations, Elizabeth's creative spirit continued to soar, culminating in the creation of a stunning masterpiece—an exquisite book chronicling her lifelong love affair with jewellery, aptly titled "Elizabeth: My Love Affair with Jewellery."

Elizabeth extended a gracious invitation to me—an opportunity to glimpse into the dazzling world of her private collection at an exclusive exhibition. It was an honour beyond measure, yet fate intervened, and I found myself unable to attend, a missed opportunity tinged with regret.

Despite her secluded existence, Elizabeth's enduring passion for beauty and elegance shone through in every page of her book—a testament to her indomitable spirit and unwavering dedication to preserving her legacy.

Charla Lawhon
Managing Editor, *In Style*

Invites you to celebrate

ELIZABETH TAYLOR
MY LOVE AFFAIR WITH JEWELRY
published by Simon & Schuster

Join Dame Elizabeth Taylor and view an exclusive exhibition of selected jewels from her legendary private collection.

Cocktail Party
Thursday, September 26th, 2002
6:30 pm to 9:30 pm
Festive cocktail attire

Christie's
20 Rockefeller Plaza
(49th Street between Fifth and Sixth Avenues)
New York City

R.S.V.P. by September 16th
212.522.8349

THIS INVITATION IS NON-TRANSFERABLE
PHOTO IDENTIFICATION REQUIRED

At the remarkable age of seventy-one, Elizabeth Taylor made a momentous decision to bid adieu to the glitz and glamour of show business—a monumental milestone marking the end of an illustrious sixty-year career.

Although slated to join a prestigious lineup of past Oscar winners for the Academy's seventy-fifth anniversary celebrations, Elizabeth gracefully declined the invitation, choosing instead to embrace a quieter, more introspective chapter of her life.

Amidst whispers of semiretirement, Elizabeth found solace in reliving the golden days of her illustrious career, surrounded by cherished friends and family. Nestled in the comfort of her home, she delighted in revisiting timeless classics like "Who's Afraid of Virginia Woolf?" and "A Place in the Sun," each film a poignant reminder of her enduring legacy on the silver screen.

Even in her moments of seclusion, Elizabeth's indomitable spirit continued to shine brightly. With the support of her dedicated personal assistants, she ventured out on occasion to attend fundraisers and accept accolades for her past and present achievements.

Among the most memorable honours was the Presidential Citizens Medal, bestowed upon her at the prestigious White House—a poignant tribute that underscored her remarkable contributions to society.

Elizabeth's trailblazing success in the fragrance industry served as a source of inspiration for countless women worldwide, igniting a trend that would captivate the hearts and senses of generations to come. In 2003, she unveiled two new fragrances, "Gardenia" and "Forever Elizabeth," each one a testament to her enduring allure and timeless elegance.

As I reflected on our cherished correspondence over the years, I couldn't help but marvel at the serendipitous connection between us. The phrase "Forever Elizabeth," which I had affectionately used to sign off our letters, had become a cherished part of our celebrity connection—a symbol of the enduring bond that transcended time and distance.

Was it mere coincidence that Elizabeth chose to immortalise this phrase in her fragrance line, or was it a secret tribute to our unwavering celebrity connection?

While the answer remained shrouded in mystery, one thing was certain— Elizabeth's profound impact on my life, and the lives of countless admirers, would endure for eternity, a testament to her enduring legacy of grace, and timeless beauty.

OSTRICH FEATHERS

This awesome black velvet clutch is masqueraded in ostrich feathers and rhinestones and has a silver-toned frame. The carry strap is decorated with pearl like embellishments This item was used when Elizabeth was maid of honour and when she attended good friend Liza Minelli's wedding in 2002.

Source: image unknown, Julien's Auctions, California.

Media reports suggested that Elizabeth was now settling into semiretirement and would often remind herself of her heyday by playing some of her old favourite movies at home with friends and family. *Who's Afraid of Virginia Woolf?* and *A Place in the Sun* were said to be among her favourites.

On the odd occasion, she would venture out, with the help of her personal assistants, to attend fundraisers and collect accolades for past and present works, including her Presidential Citizens Medal presented to her at the White House, one of the final honour ceremonies of the Bill Clinton presidency.

The success of Elizabeth's fragrances has inspired and motivated not only thousands of women worldwide but has also encouraged other celebrities to launch fragrances of their own.

In 2003, Elizabeth released two fragrances Gardenia and Forever Elizabeth.

"Forever Elizabeth" was how I had signed off on our correspondence over the years. It had become a part of my celebrity connection. I would sign, "Always and forever Elizabeth, your number one fan." Did Elizabeth coincidently recognize this phrase as ours and pay a secret tribute to my fan-ship? I like to believe so, as it wasn't like she never knew who I was or the admiration I held in my heart for her then and always.

Elizabeth signs off on what had been reported at the time as the largest memorabilia collection of its kind in the world in 2003.

Source: Albany Advertiser, Western Australia.

MEMORABILIA

In 2003, my collection of Elizabeth Taylor memorabilia was recognised by the Australian Collector's Association as being the Best Displayed collection on show and was also awarded the People's Choice Award for its pure intensity and brilliance.

At the age of seventy-four, Elizabeth Taylor's journey seemed to defy the passage of time, her life story etched with the highs and lows of fame, fortune, and enduring resilience.

Despite the whispers of her aging appearance in recent years, Elizabeth's indomitable spirit continued to captivate hearts and minds around the world, even as her once ubiquitous image faded from the glossy pages of magazines and newspapers.

Battling a lifetime of health challenges compounded by intermittent struggles with substance dependency, Elizabeth found herself the subject of sensationalized reports proclaiming her imminent demise—a surreal experience she had faced many times before.

In a remarkable display of courage and defiance, Elizabeth chose to confront these rumours head-on, making a triumphant return to television with her first interview in over four years on the Larry King show. With a steely resolve, she declared to the world that she was very much alive, dispelling the morbid speculation that had surrounded her.

In a gesture that underscored her enduring commitment to philanthropy, Elizabeth forged a historic partnership with Christie's Auction House in 2006, granting them exclusive rights to handle the future sales of her cherished jewellery, artworks, and personal memorabilia.

The proceeds from these auctions, including iconic pieces such as her 1986 Academy Award dress, would benefit the Elizabeth AIDS Foundation and the American Foundation for AIDS Research (amfAR), furthering her tireless efforts to combat the devastating effects of the disease.

As my correspondence with Elizabeth gradually dwindled to occasional letters or autographs, I felt a deep sense of reverence for her twilight years, recognizing her desire for solitude and reflection. Yet, amidst the whispers of her failing health, Elizabeth's resilience continued to shine through, defying the odds and embracing life with a renewed sense of vigour.

In July of 2008, reports of Elizabeth's hospitalization and placement on life support due to heart failure and severe pneumonia sent shockwaves around the world.

However, her publicist swiftly refuted these claims, reassuring the public that Elizabeth's health concerns were exaggerated and that her hospital visit was merely precautionary.

In a testament to her enduring spirit, Elizabeth found solace in the company of friends, often frequenting the Abbey gay bar and restaurant in California, where she savoured the simple pleasures of life, indulging in a refreshing lime daiquiri or two amidst laughter and camaraderie.

This was the last signed photograph I received from Elizabeth, and I was shocked to see her beautiful signature had resembled the scribble of an elderly lady, but unlike her written hand.

Elizabeth had aged so very gracefully—this was no act; this was Elizabeth Taylor my celebrity connection.

Source: Harry Benson/Elizabeth Taylor.

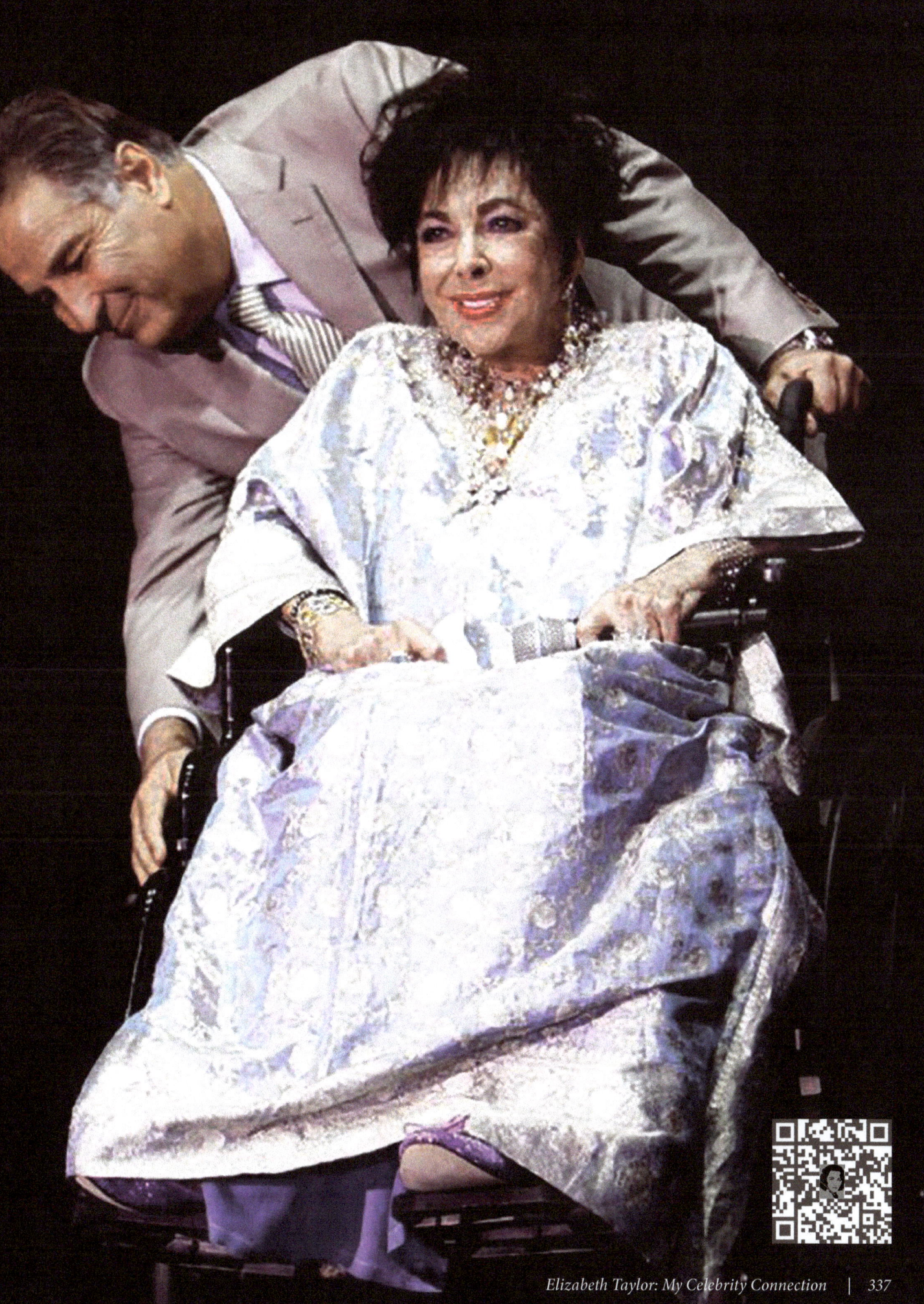

Elizabeth Taylor: My Celebrity Connection

ELIZABETH'S LAST PUBLIC OUTING

On a mild day in the hills of Bel Air, Elizabeth prepares for what will be will be her final public appearance. She is escorted to her favourite local waterhole, Abbey's Bar and Grill. Reminiscing on times gone by, Elizabeth is pictured here wearing this black Stetson cowboy hat adorned with handcrafted and embellished Native American turquoise stones.

THE LAVENDER MANUSCRIPT

In February 2010, I embarked on a momentous journey, determined to present Elizabeth with the inaugural manuscript of a book that had evolved into a true labor of love—a testament to her extraordinary life and legacy.

Originally titled "Dame Elizabeth Taylor: The Girl Who Had Everything," this manuscript represented the culmination of my lifelong passion for collecting Elizabeth memorabilia, transformed into a unique narrative that I hoped would resonate with Elizabeth and her legion of fans worldwide.

Bound in lavish lavender satin, the original 591-page manuscript embarked on a transcontinental voyage from Australia to America on February 15, 2010.

An email from House of Taylor brought news of its safe arrival on February 25, just two days before Elizabeth's seventy-eighth birthday.

Surrounding this monumental event was the passing on September 22, 2010, of Eddie Fisher at the age of eighty-two, Elizabeth's fourth husband.

In November 2010, my heart swelled with overwhelming emotion as I received Elizabeth's response to the lavender manuscript. In a world fraught with uncertainty, Elizabeth's unwavering connection to me filled me with awe and gratitude, reaffirming the enduring bond we shared despite the vast distances that separated us.

As tabloid headlines once again threatened to overshadow Elizabeth's legacy with sensationalism and speculation, I clung to hope, praying that she would defy the odds once more and emerge victorious, as she had done countless times before.

I have lived with people speculating about my health all my life and I don't say this with sarcasm, but sadly, I have outlived so many who have prematurely buried me. There are so many other things in this world to worry about and that are much more important than my health.
—Elizabeth Taylor

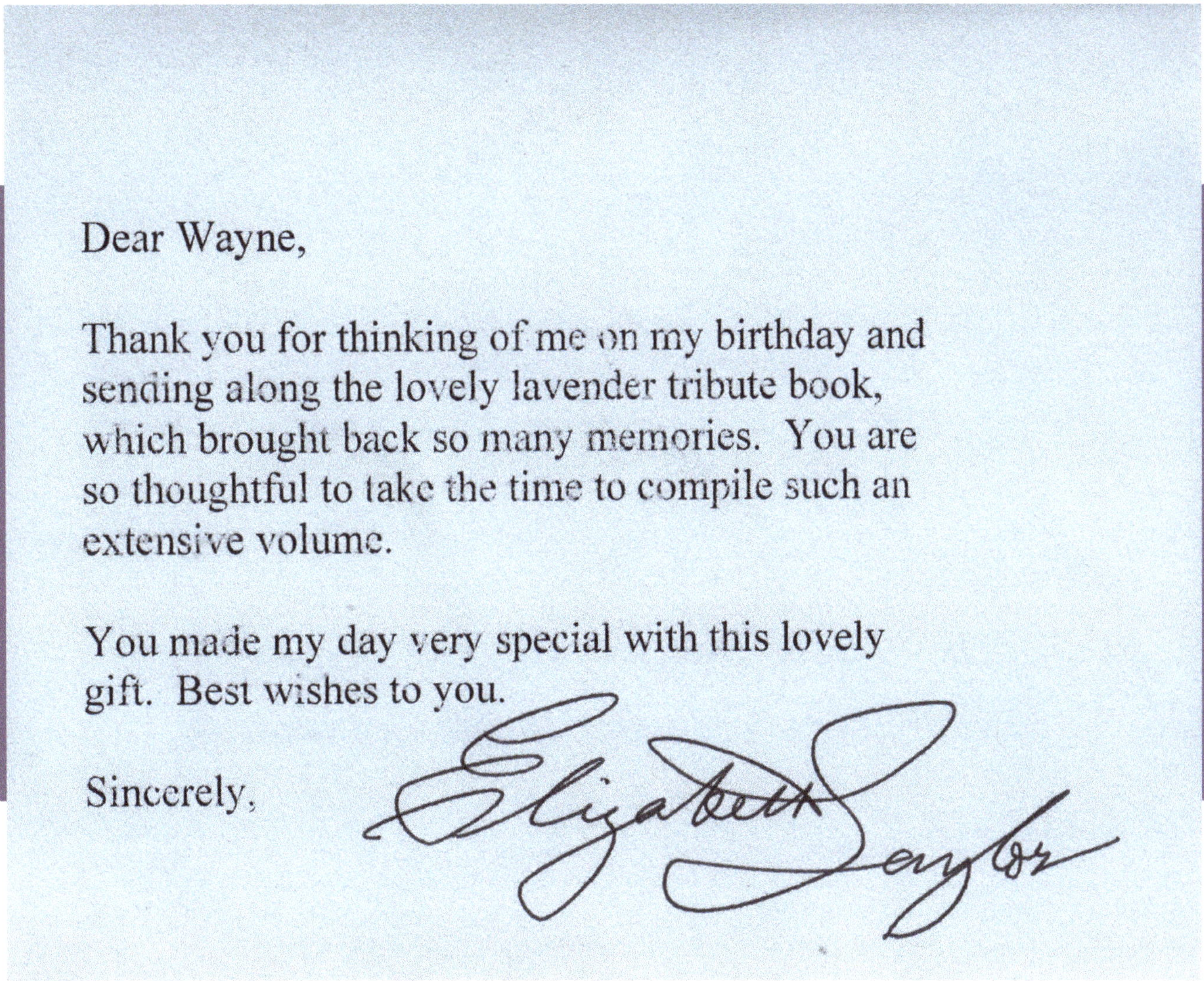

Dear Wayne,

Thank you for thinking of me on my birthday and sending along the lovely lavender tribute book, which brought back so many memories. You are so thoughtful to take the time to compile such an extensive volume.

You made my day very special with this lovely gift. Best wishes to you.

Sincerely,

Elizabeth Taylor

SUCH AN EXTENSIVE VOLUME

After viewing the original manuscript of this book, Elizabeth would write to me for the very last time on, November 20, 2010.

*If I wasn't dead every two weeks,
the tabloids wouldn't make any money.
—Elizabeth Taylor*

CEDAR-SINAI MEDICAL CENTRE

In 2011, my heart sank as I found myself glued to the Internet, anxiously scouring for updates on Elizabeth's condition. News had spread that Elizabeth had been admitted to the prestigious Cedars-Sinai Medical Centre, often dubbed the "hospital to the stars," on Friday, February 11, 2011, seeking treatment for congestive heart failure.

While reports initially hinted at her stable condition, her publicist and close family pleaded for privacy, urging fans to offer space for the medical team to work their magic.

As days stretched into weeks, the uncertainty surrounding Elizabeth's health deepened. At seventy-eight, her once formidable frame had been worn down by a litany of health battles, each leaving its mark on her resilient spirit.

From chronic back ailments stemming from childhood stardom to multiple surgeries, benign tumors, and relentless bouts of pneumonia, Elizabeth's medical journey read like a saga of endurance and resilience.

Yet, despite her indomitable spirit, Elizabeth remained confined to the hospital bed for what felt like an eternity, her seventy-ninth birthday passing by in the sterile confines of her hospital room. With each passing day, the weight of helplessness and grief grew heavier, overshadowing any glimmer of hope. Sending one last bouquet of flowers to her bedside, I couldn't shake the gnawing sense of grievance, mourning the gradual decline of a Hollywood icon whose strength had inspired generations.

March 15, 2011, marked Elizabeth's second month confined within the sterile walls of Cedars-Sinai Medical Centre. As I meticulously put the finishing touches to this book, a labor of love destined to celebrate the cherished memorabilia collection dedicated to her illustrious legacy, the cruel hand of fate dealt a devastating blow.

In the eerie silence of the early hours on March 23, 2011, a text message shattered the fragile semblance of normalcy. "Wayne, so sorry to hear about your Dearest Elizabeth," it read. Frantically, I turned to the online world for confirmation, only to be met with the heart-wrenching truth: Elizabeth Taylor, the luminous star whose presence had illuminated countless lives, had peacefully slipped away in her sleep at 1:28 a.m. (PST).

Unable to find solace in sleep, I sought refuge in the familiar embrace of "Who's Afraid of Virginia Woolf?"—a poignant reminder of the timeless bond shared between Elizabeth and Richard Burton, forever immortalized on screen.

Throughout the agonising hours that followed, my world was engulfed in a whirlwind of texts and phone calls, each a painful reminder of the profound loss echoing in my heart.

For decades, Elizabeth had been more than just a celebrity to me; she had been my confidante, my penfriend, the beacon guiding my thirty-year journey of collecting memorabilia.

Every Friday, like clockwork, her signed messages and treasured photographs would grace my letterbox, a testament to the enduring connection that had woven its way into the fabric of my life.

And now, with her passing, the void left behind was as vast and unfathomable as the starlit skies she once illuminated with her unparalleled grace.

In a final act of grace, Elizabeth Taylor, ever the cinematic icon, arrived fashionably late to her own farewell, eliciting both smiles and tears from those gathered to bid her farewell. Her resting place, nestled in the serene grounds of Forest Lawn cemetery in Glendale, California, was a testament to the swift passage of time, marked by the quiet dignity of a Jewish burial, a nod to her deep connection with husband Eddie Fisher.

As her grandson's trumpet played the haunting notes of "Amazing Grace," the world stood in solemn remembrance, mourning the loss of the last true Hollywood legend. While there was no grand public memorial, Elizabeth's enduring legacy was celebrated through a worldwide exhibition showcasing her iconic costumes and dazzling jewels, a fitting tribute to her unparalleled glamour and philanthropic spirit.

The Christie's auction, where her treasures found new homes, served as a poignant reminder of Elizabeth's unwavering commitment to her beloved AIDS charities, raising an astonishing $680 million for the Elizabeth Taylor AIDS Foundation.

Though she may have departed this world, Elizabeth's legacy continues to shine brightly, an eternal beacon of elegance and grace. Her timeless allure transcends generations, leaving an indelible mark on the hearts of her admirers worldwide. In her story of celebrity connection, she leaves behind a legacy that will forever be cherished, a testament to the enduring power of love, laughter, and compassion across galaxies untold.

Elizabeth is the best old school dame I've ever met. A regular, wonderful person, boy did I take to her, she's an astonishing great broad.

—*Johnny Depp*

We have just lost a Hollywood giant. More importantly, we have lost an incredible human being.

—*Sir Elton John*

Elizabeth's star on the Hollywood Walk of Fame is adorned with floral tributes after the world received the news of her sad passing. The Hollywood Walk of Fame comprises of more than 2,500 five-pointed terrazzo and brass stars embedded in the sidewalks along fifteen blocks of Hollywood Boulevard and three blocks of Vine Street in Hollywood, California.

Credit: RoidRanger / Shutterstock.com

Elizabeth Taylor: My Celebrity Connection | 347

IN MEMORIA

At Glendale, Elizabeth and Michael Jackson share this arch where they both now rest in peace. Elizabeth rests peacefully with a love letter from the love of her life, Richard Burton.

Source: Forest Lawn, Glendale, California/ Deidre and Gael.

Elizabeth Taylor: My Celebrity Connection | 349

In a tribute to her enduring legacy, several months after Elizabeth Taylor's passing, Christie's Auctions of New York played host to a historic event: the largest memorabilia auction in history. This extraordinary event was dedicated to honouring Elizabeth's remarkable life and supporting her lifelong mission through the Elizabeth Taylor AIDS Foundation.

The auction was nothing short of spectacular, shattering previous records and capturing the world's attention. On the first night alone, Elizabeth's treasured jewellery pieces commanded staggering sums, with sales exceeding $116 million, setting a new standard for private collections. Among the highlights was the remarkable sale of Mike Todd's diamond tiara, fetching an astonishing $4.2 million, far surpassing all expectations.

It was the legendary La Peregrina pearl that stole the spotlight, capturing hearts and imaginations alike. Adorning a necklace crafted by Cartier for Elizabeth, this sixteenth-century marvel sold for an astounding $11.8 million, setting a new world record for pearl jewels and cementing its place in history.

In a separate auction featuring items from Elizabeth's personal wardrobe, fashion enthusiasts eagerly bid on sixty-seven lots, driving the total proceeds to an impressive $2.6 million, a testament to Elizabeth's enduring influence on style and glamour.

Among the coveted pieces was the exquisite silver-encrusted Christian Dior brocade ensemble, complete with a matching purse, which fetched a remarkable $362,500, reflecting the timeless allure of Elizabeth's fashion legacy.

Source: Christie's Auctions/Elizabeth Taylor.

In the years following Elizabeth's departure, there have been several fleeting attempts to bring the magic of Elizabeth and Richard back to the silver screen, but they seemed to fade as quickly as they appeared.

One such effort was the telemovie titled "Liz and Dick," featuring the troubled actress Lindsay Lohan, which served only to emphasize the irreplaceable nature of Elizabeth's presence.

Indeed, there will never be another star whose light shines as brightly as Elizabeth's, nor another woman whose strength and dignity command such admiration.

She was a superstar like no other, genuine and incomparable.

This book, this collection, stands as a timeless tribute to the enduring admiration that the world has, and will always have, for Hollywood's beloved Dame Elizabeth Taylor.

Source: International Magazine Service (1963).

A HOMAGE TO ELIZABETH

Throughout my pen-friendship with Elizabeth, I cherished numerous opportunities to meet the Queen of Hollywood, though alas, circumstances often thwarted my plans. Then, in 2015, I resolved to pay tribute to Elizabeth Taylor in a profound way. Embarking on a pilgrimage to Los Angeles, I embarked on a journey of homage.

I began at her resting place in the Glendale Forest Lawn Memorial Park, where I stood in reverence before her gravesite. Walking along the hallowed Hollywood Walk of Fame, I felt her presence lingering in the star-studded pavement. And as I wandered through the faux gates of Bel Air, I felt as though I were treading the same paths she once did.

Arriving at her former residence, the house she inhabited until her passing, was a transcendent experience. As the gates swung open, I was enveloped in a wave of exotic fragrances—jasmine and gardenia—like an echo of Elizabeth's own presence.

Leaving a copy of this book with the new owners felt like leaving a piece of my soul behind, a symbolic embrace of the legacy Elizabeth left behind in her beloved Bel Air estate.

In the accompanying picture, the corridor of the Forest Lawn Mausoleum stands as a poignant symbol of remembrance, where both Elizabeth Taylor and Michael Jackson rest.

Elizabeth beneath the watchful gaze of a 20-foot angel, and Michael at the end of the corridor, bathed in the light of a circular glass-stained window.

ACS security services officer, Walter, permits access to the Bel Air compound. I got talking to him, and he informed me that he has been a security officer at the Bel Air compound for over twenty-five years. He went on to tell me that Elizabeth Taylor was always so pleasant and would often wave if she saw him at the faux gates.

Elizabeth's former entrance to her last place of residence,
700 Nimes Rd. Bel Air, Los Angeles, California.

ELIZABETH CELEBRATES CONNECTION

I knew then I had achieved what I had set out to achieve, so I made my way to Elizabeth's favourite bar. I sat in the same seat Elizabeth would sit during her visits to the Abbey Bar and Grill. As I ordered a cocktail made especially for Elizabeth's visit, a large ray of sunlight beamed through the coloured leadlight glass. It was like she had come to join with me in finally celebrating our connection. I was lucky enough also to acquire the recipe to a drink designed for Elizabeth and drank by her on her last visit.

Dame Elizabeth Taylor Shades of Violet

- Premium vodka 20 oz
- Kurant/ Berry Schnapps 50 oz.
- Fresh lemon juice 10 oz.
- Sugar syrup float blue curacao

Serve in large martini glass. Garnish with fresh blueberries and raspberries.

ELIZABETH: THE QUEEN OF CELEBRITY ACTIVISM

In 2017, parts of this private collection, which have been gathered over a thirty-year friendship with Elizabeth, was exhibited. Once upon a time, the word *star* applied to someone fabulous who worked in the entertainment industry. It was an accolade given to someone with magnetism, glamour, and a quality that set them apart from mere mortals. Elizabeth Taylor was in every sense of the word a superstar. Elizabeth Taylor also had a passionate commitment to fighting HIV-AIDS and, in 1985, began donating her personal income as well as raising funds to discover a cure. Today, her efforts continue posthumously and contribute significantly to the cause. The legacy of her unwavering and tireless work will surpass the likes of any Kardashian or any other wannabe celebrity heads. Elizabeth Taylor's passion in her later years was her involvement with both the American Foundation for AIDS Research and her own foundation, the Elizabeth Taylor Aids Foundation.

"It's the most important work of my life," she once said, and Elizabeth's unwavering energy proves this is no idle boast. The exhibition showcased some of Elizabeth's prized personal effects, collectable items and pieces that will give an insight into the entertainer and the activist.

A CELEBRITY CONNECTION IMMORTALISED

For eons, I combed through magazines, yearning for every morsel of Elizabeth, until I found myself perusing a catalogue brimming with relics of adoration. How close could one dare to dream from such a vast expanse?

Celebrities, both past and present, seemed beyond reach—a distant allure cloaked in the mystique of "celebrityism." Fans were granted but fleeting glimpses into their worlds, a momentary reprieve from reality.

Yet, for me, the essence of celebrity lay not in the spotlight, but in the artifacts that adorned Elizabeth's life.

Each trinket, each treasure, held a piece of her story—a glimpse into the whimsical world she curated. Elizabeth, at her core, was organic, a collector of sparkly baubles reminiscent of a bowerbird, adorning her nest with diamonds and pearls.

With each bid, I felt her presence beside me, guiding my hand towards objects that once brought her joy. Perhaps it was a picture frame cradling her beloved Sugar, or a trinket imbued with rainbow reflections, brightening her days.

But amidst my pursuit, a question lingered: what was my aim? Had my connection to celebrity, like Elizabeth herself, faded with time?

Visiting her former estate, I felt a profound sense of connection—a spiritual tether transcending time and space. As I approached 700 Nimes Road, I sensed her presence, a silent observer from afar.

Navigating through a labyrinth of opulence and wealth, I could sense her presence, whispers echoing amidst the rustle of autumn leaves. There it stood, the letterbox that once safeguarded our years of correspondence, a silent witness to our enduring bond.

Yearning to solidify my connection with celebrity, I embarked on a quest for something tangible to enrich our tale.

Envisioning relics imbued with the essence of Elizabeth Taylor's legendary lifestyle, I sought out Razor-Blade Tycoon, Rocky Malhotra, the custodian of her former estate.

Whether a humble light fixture that once bathed her visage in radiant glow or a square of lavender shag-pile carpet that cradled her every step, I longed to possess a fragment of her world.

Though Rocky seemed perplexed by my request, fate intervened when Julien's Auctions in California unveiled the "Lifestyle of Elizabeth Taylor" auction in 2019.

It was as if Elizabeth herself had heard my plea, ensuring I became the steward of her whimsical treasures.

Each fixture, each furnishing, bore witness to her touch, her gaze, her essence. In their ornate design, embellished with Austrian crystals and semi-precious stones, I found not mere objects, but relics of a profound connection—a testament to the unwavering devotion of Elizabeth Taylor's number one fan.

In that moment, I realised how effortlessly Elizabeth had woven herself into the fabric of my being.

*Isn't this what being
a celebrity is all about—
helping people?
—Elizabeth Taylor*

*Give, remember always give.
That is the thing that
will make you grow.
— Elizabeth Taylor*

700 NIMES ROAD

Nimes Road, a winding pathway leading to the pinnacle of Bel Air, holds within its bends the echoes of Elizabeth Taylor's illustrious journey. For three decades, she traversed these hallowed grounds, leaving an indelible mark upon the landscape until her final farewell in 2011.

Behind the guarded gates, the legendary movie star and tireless activist resided, her abode a sanctuary where she shared laughter, love, and the simple joys of life with her cherished circle.

Amidst the fragrant blooms of gardenias and lilies of the valley, she found solace, often stealing moments beneath her arbor, savouring the tranquillity over a cup of tea.

Within these walls, dreams took flight, and from the depths of her soul emerged the essence of inspiration, culminating in the creation of the world's most beloved fragrance for women. Her legacy transcended mere celebrity, becoming a beacon of hope in the global fight against AIDS.

In her final days, Elizabeth entrusted interior designer Waldo Fernandez to craft her private haven into a haven of opulence and elegance. Lavender carpets kissed the floors, embroidered silk wallpaper adorned the walls, and a bespoke mirrored display cabinet housed her treasured accolades, including her three coveted Oscar statues.

Nimes Road stands not only as a testament to Elizabeth's unparalleled grace and beauty but as a timeless tribute to her enduring spirit and boundless generosity.

Since 2011, Elizabeth's legendary Bel Air abode has changed hands twice, the latest exchange occurring in 2022 through an off-market transaction with property developer Ardie Tavangarian.

Yet, as these words are penned, the remnants of Elizabeth Taylor's once-vibrant lifestyle are being dismantled. The new owner's blueprint entails razing the historic structure to make way for a garish, cookie-cutter mansion—a decision that reeks of disrespect.

There's an undeniable injustice in this act. This was the hallowed ground where the trailblazing actress and pioneering AIDS activist once roamed. Now, the only tangible reminder of Elizabeth's presence will be digital echoes of her private sanctuary scattered across the vast expanse of cyberspace.

Whatever monstrosity arises from the whims of the affluent, no edifice of brick, mortar, or towering windows can ever replace the boundless compassion and goodwill that Elizabeth Taylor bestowed upon the world.

Her words, echoing from her portrayal of Cleopatra, ring with resounding truth: "How DARE you and the rest of your barbarians set fire to my library?

Play conqueror all you want, Mighty Caesar! Rape, murder, pillage thousands, even millions of human beings! But neither you nor any other barbarian has the right to destroy one human thought!"

Source: Google Maps/ Blogspot

Elizabeth Taylor: My Celebrity Connection | 367

*Thank you for sharing in the life
that was Elizabeth Taylor
and my celebrity connection.
I hope that you too
will keep true to the legacy
that was and will always be
Elizabeth Taylor.*

—Wayne Griffin

SOME MORE PHOTOGRAPHIC CREDITS

Tom Wargacki - Nancy Barr - Seuss Filtio

Ralph Merlino - Charles Moniz - Brad Darrach

Robert Cohen - Lou Valentino - Erika Davidson

Joe Decker – Neal Peters- Nat Gallinger

Yani Begakis - Elis McCarthy - Reed Cohen

Frank Teti - Kevin Winter - Chris Hunter

Herb Ritts -Bob Scott - James Smeal

Peter Brandt - Alex Berliner - Cal Gleason

Gene Daniels - Henry Pessar - Marcus Adams

Beverly Carr - Nancy Barr -Sam Emerson

Bruce Weber- Harry Winston - Floyd McCarty

Felice Quinto - Clarence S Bull - Danny Eccleston

Raimondo Borea - Jack Buxbaun - Michael Tullberg

Ethan Miller- Vincent Yu Slug- Fred Guiol.

A SPECIAL MENTION

Star Wares, Celebrity Seconds, Heritage Auction House, Julien's Auction House, and Fraser's Autographs, George Houlle Books and autographs, Video Connection, Wholesale video supplies, Warner Home Video. Communication and Entertainment limited, Hoyts Polygram Video, Road show home video library, Columbia Pictures, Twentieth Century Fox, Stars, Rock and Movie Posters.

Museum of moving images London, The Silver Screen Archives, London Daily Mirror, Paris Match, Annan Photo Features, NBC, HBO, ABC Photographs, Reuters, Getty Images, Foto- Ad Inc, M.G.M, United Press Limited, Cine-Arte, Mirror pic, Associated Press, Wide World Photo's, Cinelandia, 20th Century Fox, Universal Pictures, Paramount Pictures, Pictorial Parade, Daily News, Authenticated Inc, Propiedad Tito Franco, B & H Productions, House Of Taylor, Elizabeth Arden Inc, Christie's Auction House, Vivid Images Inc, Chen Sam & Associates, Movie Heaven, Long Photographs, Ron Galella Limited, La Scalia Autographs.

American Foundation for AIDS research, Elizabeth AIDS Foundation, Madam Alexander's, Franklin Mint, Turner Entertainment, Time Life Inc, Examiner Magazine, National Enquirer, The Earliest Bird, Google Earth, Andy Warhol, Harmonie Autographs and Music International, La Scala Autographs Inc, Foto.com, APF Annan Photo Features.

Keystone/Getty Images, Big Pictures, Barcroft Media, Australasian Picture Library, Austral, Perfumes International, Wire Images, PA/ Reuters, Blitz Pictures, Nikos, Image Bank, The Photo Library, Picture Media, Alpha Globe Photos, Snap /Rev Features, London Entertainment/ Splash News, Snapper Media, FotoPics, Classic Graphics and Changing Posters.

By: Wayne Griffin

www.ingramcontent.com/pod-product-compliance
Lightning Source LLC
Chambersburg PA
CBHW042351070526
44585CB00028B/2890